THE KHRUSH

Studies in European History

Genral Editor: Richard Overy
Editorial Consultants: John Breuilly
Roy Porter

PUBLISHED TITLES

FORTHCOMING

THE KHRUSHCHEV ERA

De-Stalinisation and the Limits of
Reform in the USSR, 1953–1964

DONALD FILTZER

150th YEAR
M
MACMILLAN

First published 1993 by
THE MACMILLAN PRESS LTD
Houndmills, Basingstoke, Hampshire RG21 2XS
and London
Companies and representatives
throughout the world

ISBN 0–333–58526–7

A catalogue record for this book is available
from the British Library

Printed in Hong Kong

Series Standing Order

If you would like to receive future titles in this series as they are published, you
can make use of our standing order facility. To place a standing order please
contact your bookseller or, in case of difficulty, write to us at the address below
with your name and address and the name of the series. Please state with which
title you wish to begin your standing order. (If you live outside the ·United
Kingdom we may not have the rights for your area, in which case we will
forward your order to the publisher concerned.)

Customer Services Department, Macmillan Distribution Ltd.
Houndmills, Basingstoke, Hampshire, RG21 2XS, England.

Contents

List of Russian Terms
Used in the Text

Gosplan	State Planning Commission
intelligentsia	In modern usage all those with higher education, but also used in its pre-revolutionary sense to refer to the liberal intellectuals, that is, writers, artists, musicians, etc.
KGB	Committee for State Security, in charge of the secret police
kolkhoz	collective farm
kolkhoznik	collective farm member
Komsomol	Communist Youth League, the youth wing of the Communist Party
MTS	Machine Tractor Station (on a collective farm)
MVD	Ministry of Internal Affairs. Prior to Stalin's death the secret police were under the Ministry of State Security, which was briefly merged with the MVD under Beria's control after Stalin died. Later in 1953, after Beria's ouster, the secret police were placed under the newly-created KGB.
obkom	Regional Committee of the Communist Party (short for *Oblast'* Committee)
oblast'	region or province, the main administrative unit within a Republic
raikom	District Committee of the Communist Party (short for *Raion* Committee)
raion	district (within a city or an *oblast'*)
sovkhoz	state (literally, Soviet) farm
sovkhoznik	state farm worker
sovnarkhoz	literally, Council of the National Economy, more commonly known as Regional Economic Council

Organisation of the Communist Party and the Soviet Government

Until Gorbachev introduced an elected Parliament in 1989 and an executive presidency in 1990, the government of the USSR was dominated by the Communist Party. The main features of the organisation of Party and government are shown in the following diagram. The diagram is laid out to show the rough equivalence between Party and government bodies at each territorial level.

PARTY	GOVERNMENT
Presidium (later known as the Politburo)	Presidium of the USSR Council of Ministers
Central Committee of the Communist Party of the Soviet Union	USSR Council of Ministers
Congress of the Communist Party of the Soviet Union	{ Presidium of the USSR Supreme Soviet USSR Supreme Soviet
Republic Secretariat	Republic Council of Ministers
Republic Party Central Committee	Presidium of Republic Supreme Soviet
Republic Party Congress	Republic Supreme Soviet
Regional (*oblast'*) Party Committee Regional (*oblast'*) Party Conference }	City Soviet/Regional (*oblast'*) Soviet
Lower Party Bodies (district, etc.) Lower Party Conferences }	District/Village Soviet
Primary Party Organisations (factory, collective farm, etc.)	[No governmental equivalent]
Rank and file Party members	Voting Population

Explanation

Party: Unlike governmental bodies, Party bodies were chosen via a system of indirect election, with each body electing delegates to the next higher rung in the hierarchy. Lower Party bodies (district, etc.) elected delegates to the Regional (*oblast'*) Conferences. The Regional Conferences in turn elected delegates to the Republic Party Congresses. Each Republic Party Congress elected its own Central Committee, which selected its own Secretariat to run the day-to-day Party business in the Republic. Both the Republic Party Congresses *and* the Regional (*oblast'*) Party Conferences elected delegates to the Congress of the Communist Party of the Soviet Union. This Congress elected a Central Committee for the entire Party, which selected a Politburo (in Khrushchev's time known as the Presidium) to see to its ongoing affairs.

Government: The voting population of the USSR in theory directly 'elected' deputies to the soviets at all levels of government, from the local district soviets up to the Supreme Soviets of Republics and the USSR. Local soviets elected Executive Committees to run their day-to-day business. The larger bodies, that is, the Republican and USSR Supreme Soviets, each elected a Presidium to manage their daily affairs, and a Council of Ministers, which functioned as a cabinet, with Ministers in charge of the main branches of the economy and the government.

In reality there was little or no selection from the bottom up: lower appointments (e.g., Central Committee members, *oblast'* Party secretaries, members of Republic or USSR Councils of Ministers, etc.) were selected by the Communist Party in Moscow. Also, the Supreme Soviet had no real power at either Republic or national level. The Council of Ministers had real power, but only insofar as its members belonged to the Communist Party and executed Party policy.

viii

List of Maps and Acknowledgements

Map 1 is reproduced with the permission of Yale University Press, from *An Atlas of Russian History*, 1970. Maps 2 and 3 are reproduced with the permission of George Weidenfeld & Nicolson Ltd, from Martin Gilbert, *The Russian History Atlas*.

Map 1   The USSR circa 1960

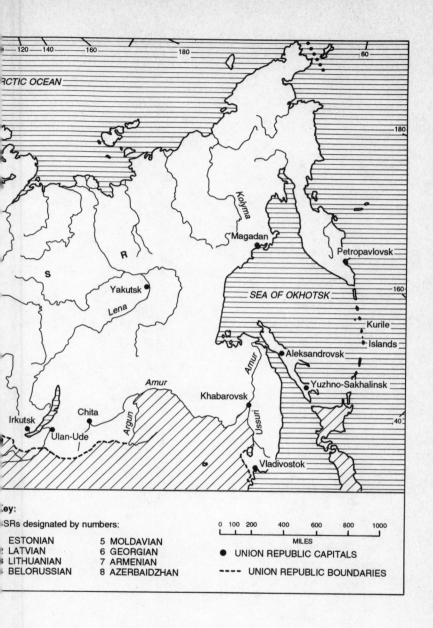

Preface

No event has dominated world history during the past ten years more than the transformation and break-up of the Soviet Union under Mikhail Gorbachev. Gorbachev's was not the first major attempt to reform the Soviet system. Some 30 years before, Nikita Khrushchev had launched a series of far-reaching, although generally unsuccessful efforts to reshape the Stalinist system and replace it with something less oppressive and more humane. The parallels between Khrushchev and Gorbachev are in many ways quite striking. Both men came to power not as head of state, but by virtue of their appointment as General Secretary (called First Secretary in Khrushchev's day) of the Soviet Communist Party, a position which they skilfully used to increase their personal power and advance their programmes for change. Both were keenly aware that the country they headed was in a period of economic and political crisis, not the least because of profound popular discontent with a low standard of living and a lack of political freedom. Finally, Khrushchev and Gorbachev each realised that they had both an opportunity and a problem. They were now in charge, and so had the chance to try to reverse the situation. But they also knew that this would challenge the power and the privileges of the Communist Party apparatus, the very people who had to approve their reform programmes at the top levels of government and implement them at all levels of national and local administration. Equally important, if the reforms went too far, they would undermine the foundations of the system from which they themselves drew their power. In short, each was faced with a dilemma: how to reform the Soviet system without going so far that the system itself came tumbling down.

Not surprisingly, Gorbachev moved cautiously at first. By his own admission, he first thought that it would be enough to restructure the economy, allowing enterprises greater freedom and reducing the power of the central planners. Soon, however, he came to realise that without drastic political reforms his economic programme would

1

come to nothing. If people did not feel that they had some say in the political system and some control over how their enterprises and local councils were governed, they would not make any effort to do better at the work place either. Gorbachev came to the conclusion that economic reform and political reform had to go hand in hand [84: *228*]. He therefore began by taking small steps to alter the political complexion of the Communist Party's Central Committee and Politburo. Then, in 1988, he became a bit bolder and announced that the following year there would be elections to a genuine Parliament. Even this reform was a half-measure, because the new election laws still gave undue advantage to the Party apparatus. Even so, when the elections occurred in March 1989 the Soviet electorate showed considerable sophistication, turning many hard-line Party leaders out of office in favour of independent candidates. Later elections to local councils and Republican parliaments gave the independents an even stronger showing [31: *111–43*].

By the end of 1991, when the Soviet Union broke up and Gorbachev fell from power, the country looked nothing like it had in 1985. There was an elected parliament. People enjoyed basic civil liberties undreamed of under previous rulers, such as freedom of speech, the right to strike, and the right to hold political demonstrations. The press was relatively free to print what it wanted. And there were important attempts to move away from the old system of economic management based on ultra-centralised, bureaucratic planning. Internationally the Soviet Union willingly accepted – and probably even initiated – the break-up of its system of 'satellite' countries in Eastern Europe and entered into new diplomatic relations and arrangements with the major industrialised capitalist countries. People commonly talked about the end of the Cold War. Indeed, the Russian terms *glasnost'* (publicity, or the act of making something known) and *perestroika* (reconstruction), the by-words of Gorbachev's reform campaigns, became household words around the globe.

However momentous these changes were, the reforms had not proceeded smoothly or in the way that Gorbachev had hoped or planned. Up until 1990 Gorbachev and his reform colleagues still insisted that in the new Soviet Union people would have a great deal of political and personal freedom, but the Communist Party would continue to hold a monopoly of political power. In other words, the system would become more efficient with greater popular trust, but the privileges of the ruling group would remain intact. Events showed this to be an impossible task. Many of the Republican Parliaments, including that of the Russian Federation, the largest Republic in the USSR, became dominated by reformers who wanted faster moves towards a market. Several republics, in particular the Baltic states of Lithuania, Latvia, and Estonia, demanded independence from Moscow. Even before it was banned in the wake of the August 1991 *putsch*, the importance of the Communist Party had declined to the point where it was about to split into rival groups. The power of its officials at both national and local level had in places almost disappeared. The economy was in serious trouble, and in many ways was even worse off than when Gorbachev took control. Food and basic consumer items were scarcer in 1991 than at any time since the early 1970s. Production was falling. People openly voiced their discontent with the fall in their standard of living and the slowness of political change. Large tracts of the economy became dominated by organised criminals, and by state bureaucrats and factory managers who had 'bought up' their enterprises as their own private property. The rise of nationalism in the USSR's separate Republics had already made it doubtful that the Soviet Union would even continue to exist as a centralised state.

The Khrushchev reforms followed a rather different path. Khrushchev, as we shall see, was a controversial figure whose place in history is far from settled. He came to power shortly after Stalin's death in 1953 and was ousted by his colleagues in the Communist Party's ruling Presidium in October 1964. He thus became the first Soviet leader to be removed peacefully from office, a fact which some historians have taken as evidence of the profound change his reforms brought to the Soviet system [22: *206*; 11: *284*]. His reforms were truly ambitious. He completely overhauled the organisation of both industry and agriculture, introduced major changes in the structure and functioning of the Communist Party, reformed the educational system and the provision of social welfare, and undertook a massive house-building campaign. More importantly, he attacked Stalin and dismantled the worst aspects of the terror through which Stalin had ruled. Yet for all this effort and energy Khrushchev's reforms brought surprisingly little change to Soviet society. He ended Stalin's terror and emptied the labour camps, but he did not introduce general political freedom and was even quite willing bloodily to suppress popular demonstrations and protests, such as those in the city of

Novocherkassk in 1962. He tried to streamline the creaking inefficiency of the Stalinist planning system and give the peasants greater incentives to produce more food. Although the standard of living rose from the appallingly low levels of the Stalin years, he merely replaced one set of bureaucratic arrangements with another and so never overcame the economic difficulties this system created. Khrushchev may, in the words of Mark Frankland, have 'left his country a better place than he found it' [22: *209*], but it was still a system that, under his successors, fell all too easily into a state of economic, social, and political stagnation.

In the West during the 1960s and early 1970s there were many books written about Khrushchev, mostly from the point of view of traditional 'Kremlinology', looking at the ins and outs of power relations within the Soviet political system. Then in 1977 the brothers Roy and Zhores Medvedev published an outstanding comprehensive analysis of the Khrushchev years [52], followed in 1982 by Roy Medvedev's longer biography [50]. Both drew on many sources not available in the West. But it was the prospect of change in the USSR, in particular the advent of *perestroika* and *glasnost'*, which really revived interest in Khrushchev, both in his own country [60; 35; 7; 75] and abroad [56; 45]. People were intrigued by the parallels between de-Stalinisation and *perestroika* and were anxious to know if Gorbachev would be astute enough to avoid many of Khrushchev's mistakes. There has, therefore, been a modest reappraisal of the Khrushchev years: indeed, several of the sources used in this book were first presented as papers to international conferences called precisely to reassess Khrushchev's importance in the light of the changes taking place under Gorbachev [46; 24]. The aim of this book is partly to continue this task. In the main, however, it seeks to answer two questions. What were Khrushchev's reforms, and why did they fail? In dealing with these questions we shall be looking not so much at Khrushchev as an individual leader, as at the structural features of the Soviet system which made that society so resistant to change.

The idea to write the book came in 1986, while teaching a unit on post-war Soviet History to A-Level students at Pimlico School in London, and I am grateful to Helen O'Malley, Head of History at the school, for inviting me back to work with several succeeding years of Pimlico students using a rough draft of the text. Robert Service and

4

Richard Overy both gave generously of their time reading later drafts and offering detailed comments and suggestions for revision. It is safe to say that, thanks to their efforts, the book is a far more solid piece of history writing than otherwise would have been the case. Thanks are also due to the Leverhulme Trust, which financed a major research project, culminating in the publication of my detailed study of labour conditions in the Khrushchev period, *Soviet Workers and De-Stalinization* (Cambridge University Press, 1962). Much of the research done for that book has in different ways found its way into the present work. Needless to say, none of those mentioned here are responsible for its remaining errors or shortcomings.

1 Introduction: The Problem of Reform in the Post-Stalin Era

When Stalin died in March 1953 he left behind a country in a deep state of crisis. The economy, despite the country's fairly rapid recovery from the destruction caused by World War II, was in a terrible state. Industry and agriculture were both hopelessly inefficient and the standard of living was low [21: *1*]. Politically, the system of controlling the population through terror had clearly outlived its usefulness. Even during the last years of Stalin's life there were numerous revolts among prisoners in the labour camps, some of which had proven difficult to put down [29: *327–32*]. Restrictive measures affecting the 'free' population, for example, the 1940 law which made absenteeism from work and job-changing criminal offences, had also become counter-productive, and both industrial managers and the lower courts had become reluctant to enforce them [21: *36–8*; 23: *22*]. Within the more narrow political arena of the Communist Party and the government administration, it was evident that the political machinery needed revitalisation. In the last years of Stalin's reign decision-making had rested almost exclusively with Stalin and a handful of people around him. The Central Committee had not met for several years; the Presidium of the Central Committee, which was supposed to see to the day-to-day running of the country, met infrequently; and the Nineteenth Party Congress of 1952 – allegedly the country's highest policy-making body – was called and convened only after a delay of nearly 14 years [71: *237–8*]. Even in a system as centralised and authoritarian as the USSR, it was simply impossible to organise and run a large and complex economy and society with decision-making concentrated in the hands of so few people. Stalin, being ever fearful of possible rivals, had intentionally made no provision for a transition to a new leadership in the event of his death. Thus, when he died, a hastily-convened meeting of the USSR's top leaders decided that, for the moment at least, power

6

should pass to a Presidium of the Communist Party's Central Committee, consisting of 10 men [52: *2*; 70: *558*]. Of these, six were more powerful than the others, and it was they who entered into a struggle to become Stalin's successor.

Lavrenti Beria, like Stalin, was a native Georgian and had risen to prominence during the Purges and the terror of the 1930s. At the time of Stalin's death he was head of the Ministry of State Security, which meant he also controlled the dreaded secret police. During the first days of the post-Stalin succession he was also made head of the Ministry of Internal Affairs, known by its Russian initials as MVD. This position naturally gave him enormous power and he was genuinely feared by his rivals [52: *2–3*].

V. M. Molotov had been an associate of Stalin's from the early 1920s and had helped engineer his rise to power. In the 1930s he was Chair of the Council of People's Commissars (in effect the Soviet Cabinet) and then Foreign Minister (he negotiated and signed the Stalin-Hitler non-aggression pact before the outbreak of World War II). Although perhaps Stalin's longest-serving ally, his political importance had diminished after the war, and Stalin had not made him part of his inner Cabinet after the Nineteenth Communist Party Congress in 1952 [49: *82–112*].

Lazar Kaganovich had also been a long-standing associate of Stalin's from the 1920s and had been part of Stalin's inner circle from 1930 onwards [49: *113–39*].

K. E. Voroshilov was another of Stalin's close comrades-in-arms, having been a member of the Politburo since 1926 and Commissar (Minister) for Defence since 1925 [49: *1–27*].

G. M. Malenkov was probably the most powerful leader after Stalin's death. He had been a key figure in the Purges of 1936–1938 and a member of the ruling Politburo since 1946. At the Nineteenth Communist Party Congress in 1952 he delivered the Central Committee Report on behalf of Stalin, who was too weak to make the speech himself. After Stalin's death he became Chair of the Council of Ministers (in effect the Prime Minister), and was considered the leading candidate to become the USSR's top ruler [49: *140–63*].

Nikita Sergeevich Khrushchev became the new Party First Secretary. He was possibly the least influential of the contenders, and certainly the person considered least likely to challenge the others for power.

Few people looking at Khrushchev's biography would have predicted that he would introduce major reforms of the Stalinist system. Khrushchev was born in 1894, in Kalinovka, in Kursk *oblast'*, the son of peasants. He became active in Bolshevik politics at an early age, and trained and worked as a fitter in the coal mines of Ukraine. After the October Revolution and Civil War he attended a mining institute in Moscow, but after graduating went into full-time politics, as Secretary of a Party district committee (*raikom*) in a coal-mining area of Ukraine. From there he worked his way up in Party circles until in the mid-1930s he was made First Secretary of the Moscow City Communist Party and direct deputy to Kaganovich. He also joined the Party's Central Committee. From there, in 1938, he went back to Ukraine as head of the Ukrainian Party, where he remained, save for a brief demotion following the War, until being recalled to Moscow in late 1949 and eventually being appointed to the Party Presidium (the old Politburo) by Stalin in 1952 [50; 69: *39–53*].

The most important thing about Khrushchev's background was that he was a product of the Stalinist system. He belonged to that generation of Communists who had advanced into positions of authority precisely as a result of the Great Purges of the 1930s. When the core of old Bolsheviks who had made the October Revolution were removed from their posts, shot, or imprisoned, it was Khrushchev and thousands like him who took their place. The Stalinist system also schooled him in the rules of political survival: how to be shrewd, subservient when necessary, and how to intrigue against one's opponents. Yet he brought to this background his own personal characteristics. He was energetic and, in his own way, highly idealistic. He believed in the Soviet system. But he was also impatient and impetuous. In his last years in office, as his various reforms foundered, he almost desperately hopped from one ill-thought-out shake-up to another. He also became, in Roy Medvedev's words, 'a bully . . . less and less self-critical, compounding his mistakes by refusing to acknowledge his failures' [50: *ix*].

At the time of Stalin's death, however, there was nothing in Khrushchev's career to suggest that he had been anything but a loyal Stalinist. In his memoirs he quite frankly describes his subservience to Stalin during these years and his acquiescence – if not participation – in the Purges that destroyed so many Party workers and ordinary citizens in the 1930s [34: *343*]. Yet it was Khrushchev who eventually launched the major reforms that have come to be known as 'de-Stalinisation'.

8

It would be wrong, however, to assume that somehow Khrushchev stood alone against the rest of Stalin's old guard, trying to acquire enough power and influence to launch his secret programme for change. The extent of the economic, political, and social crisis at the time Stalin died was so great that all the contenders for power saw the need for change and advocated reform programmes. Ironically, Beria, the feared and ruthless head of the secret police, appeared as the most reform-minded of the new leadership. Moreover, most of them recognised that at the heart of the country's problems lay the low morale of the population. Society simply could no longer bear the strain of living under constant terror. But the problem of morale went far deeper, striking at the root of the society's ability to function. This expressed itself most clearly in the country's poor labour productivity (that is, the amount that each individual could produce in industry, agriculture or services). The Polish economist W. Brus (now living and teaching in Britain) has noted that, although the post-Stalin reforms (especially those of Khrushchev) had larger political motives, the main problem they set out to solve was *how to improve productivity* and people's incentives to work. Essentially, Stalin's successors all recognised that the Soviet Union continued to show poor economic performance not just because of the destruction caused by World War II (indeed, the USSR brought production back to pre-war levels surprisingly quickly), but because of popular dissatisfaction with the Stalinist system and people's low motivation at work which resulted from it [6: *112–21*]. The dilemma this posed the regime was well summed up at the time by Edward Crankshaw, the *Observer* Soviet affairs correspondent during Khrushchev's rule [10: *60–1*].

What is important, however, is that the post-Stalin reforms, or some of them, were inevitable. The problem facing the new leadership, collective or individual, was how to massage life back into the numbed limbs of society, how to encourage the new vitality to express itself and fructify, and how, at the same time, keep it within bounds, so that the whole elaborate edifice of administration was not swept away.

Terror and coercion were no longer effective. People would have to be persuaded and coaxed into performing better at the workplace. This was a problem that could not be solved solely within the economy, even though its most immediate symptoms were economic.

9

Granted, Khrushchev did make sweeping changes in the organisation and management of the economy, in the shop floor position of industrial workers, and in agricultural conditions. But Khrushchev and the people around him saw that in order to improve morale and with it labour productivity, they would have to liberalise and reform wider aspects of Soviet life.

As we shall see in the next section, Khrushchev was not the only one to perceive the need to criticise Stalin, either. What differentiated him from the others, however, was that he had been less deeply involved in the terror of the 1930s and its maintenance after the War. Thus his hands appeared to be less bloody, so he could go farther in this criticism than the others. He proved also to be more politically astute both at assessing the prevailing mood among younger Communist Party officials and at building a base of support for himself inside the Party. In the end if Khrushchev became the author of de-Stalinisation it was partially because he had a clearer and bolder vision of the need for reforms than did his rivals, and partly because, as the one who actually won the power struggle after 1953, he was in the position to implement a reform programme and they were not.

As we shall see, most of Khrushchev's reforms in fact failed to achieve the results that were expected. In general we can identify four main reasons why this occurred:

1. Some reforms failed because they were badly thought out or poorly prepared, even where they were well-intentioned and addressed real difficulties. Khrushchev, especially in the later years of his rule, was constantly being accused of pursuing 'hare-brained schemes'.

2. Some reforms failed because the Soviet system could not 'digest' them. In other words, the cumbersomeness of the Soviet bureaucracy and the country's economic backwardness undermined the new policies and either prevented their implementation or distorted their results.

3. Some reforms failed because sections of the Communist Party or government bureaucracy felt threatened by them and resisted or distorted their implementation.

4. Finally, some reforms failed because Khrushchev and the rest of the Communist Party leadership, like the officials below them, were willing to liberalise economic and political life only insofar as this did not threaten their own ruling position. Thus the

policies they followed were not nearly as radical as what was actually needed to solve the problems the country faced.

When we look at the individual reforms we shall see that their failures usually were due to an interaction of two or more of these four factors. The end result was that the various reforms tended to create new problems that were often as bad as, or worse than, the problems they had set out to solve. The one exception was the break-up of Stalin's labour camps and the release of millions of victims of Stalin's terror. It is no accident that most Soviet citizens, in particular the intelligentsia (whom Khrushchev otherwise often harassed), were willing to forgive Khrushchev many of his failures since, in their eyes, this reform towered above all others. On the other hand, a more detached analysis of even this aspect of de-Stalinisation shows that it was quite limited.

2 The Background to De-Stalinisation: The Events of 1953

Even before Stalin's death the need for economic and even some political reforms had been mooted. Malenkov, it is true, had blocked any discussion of economic reforms at the Nineteenth Party Congress in 1952 [49: *153*]. But in 1949 Khrushchev, the only Soviet leader with any first-hand experience of rural life and with even the slightest inkling of the desperate situation in the countryside, was made Politburo spokesman for agricultural affairs and managed to push through some limited improvements in that area, primarily through a policy of amalgamating smaller and bankrupt (or nearly bankrupt) collective farms (*kolkhozy*) with more prosperous farms [52: *32–3*; 55: *115*]. Perhaps more significantly, Khrushchev claimed that local party organisations (see, the Organisation of the Communist Party and Soviet Government, p. vii) needed revitalisation and should hold plenary sessions (that is, sessions of all their members) at regular intervals [71: *235*]. Presumably even at this early date Khrushchev recognised that morale even among Party members was low and would improve only if they felt themselves more involved in local affairs.

Immediately after Stalin's death there were cautious movements towards de-Stalinisation. The regime began emphasising the need for 'socialist legality', that is, an end to arbitrary arrests and administration of justice, and their replacement by the allegedly impartial rule of law. There were warnings against the 'cult of personality', a term that was to become a euphemism for the hero worship that Stalin had created around himself. Some economic and political reforms were cautiously being floated, but all within the context of maintaining loyalty to Stalin while at the same time implying some criticism [71]. Perhaps surprisingly, in view of later

12

events, Khrushchev was not the main champion of these reforms. Malenkov attempted to cement his position as Stalin's heir by offering the population lower food prices and a shift of resources into consumer goods industries [63: *323–4*]. He also put himself forward as champion of the intellectual thaw that followed Stalin's death [8: *248*]. Even more 'radical' were the reform proposals of Beria, whose own campaign for the leadership proved extremely brief.

On 26 June 1953 there was the so-called Beria affair, where Beria was arrested and summarily executed for allegedly planning to seize power using the troops of his Ministry of Internal Affairs (MVD) [50: *56–62*]. The accusations are probably true, although we cannot know for certain; it is certainly the case that Beria was ruthless and capable of trying to stage a *coup d'état* (although the charge that he was a British agent was clearly untrue). Yet, as improbable as it may seem, Beria had been seen as the reformer within the leadership. Isaac Deutscher, the great historian and biographer of both Stalin and Trotsky, wrote at the time that he considered Beria to be the main 'de-Staliniser' against the old guard [15; 17: *147–8*]. There was some basis for this view. Beria had advocated a radical reorganisation of agriculture to ease the heavy burdens on the peasantry, had proposed relaxing the Soviet Union's hold on Eastern Europe, in particular East Germany, and proposed less repressive control over the non-Russian nationalities within the USSR [71: *236*; 72: *290–5*]. Nevertheless, when Molotov and Malenkov joined Khrushchev in the move to oust Beria their main worry was not his reform programme, but the threat that he might use his control of the MVD to advance his drive for power. The threat of a Beria coup was real. Combined with the possible unrest that his allegedly 'radical' reforms might cause, this threat prompted Khrushchev, Molotov and Malenkov to act.

In July 1953 there was a Plenum (the same as a plenary session) of the Central Committee. This Plenum marks the first major step towards de-Stalinisation. First, the leadership admitted that the country was facing grave economic difficulties. Whole industries were said to be backward. Industry was unable to supply agriculture with equipment or to satisfy the 'material and cultural' requirements of the urban population (Soviet code words for saying the standard of living was appallingly low). Agriculture itself was in a disastrous state. The grain harvest – usually the subject of much boasting at such gatherings, even if the figures had to be falsified to justify it – was

13

not even mentioned. Livestock and horticulture (fruit and vegetable growing) were said to need speedy and massive support. A good number of *kolkhozy* and entire rural regions were so badly off that the populations were abandoning them. These economic troubles were linked to political 'irregularities', for example, the delay in calling the Nineteenth Party Congress, the fact that the Central Committee had not met for several years, the infrequent meetings of the Presidium, and the absence of collective discussions of policy [71].

Although the report of the Plenum pointed the finger at Stalin, there was still no open criticism. Instead everything was fantastically blamed on Beria. However, in off-the-record meetings with foreign Communists some of Stalin's failings were pointed out; but there was still no systematic critique of Stalin's behaviour and no criticism of any of his actions before the late 1940s. The 1930s and the height of the Stalinist terror were not even mentioned. Nevertheless, the July Plenum marked a major turning point. It also led to some practical results. The MVD was split up and replaced by the Committee for State Safety (Russian initials KGB), which in turn was deprived of its independence and put back under Party control, so that no single person should again be able to use it as a power base [50: *68–9*]. Also, 1954 and 1955 saw the release of several thousand political prisoners, a small sum compared to the several million released after Khrushchev's attack on Stalin at the Twentieth Party Congress in 1956, but nonetheless the beginning of what was to become an unstoppable process [52: *19*].

The question is, how is it that Molotov, Malenkov and Khrushchev, each of whom was competing for power against the others, were able to agree on a joint position as they did at the July Plenum? Despite the disagreements and rivalries between them, all concurred that the Soviet state, its economy, and society were in a state of crisis and that urgent changes had to be made if disaster was to be avoided. This realisation came to them within weeks, not months, of Stalin's death and was the cement holding together their temporary alliance.

The Presidium had *used* the Beria affair to justify reform. The Presidium knew that it could no longer rely on terror and would have to depend more heavily on persuasion to motivate the population. The problem was how to abandon Stalin's policies without a reappraisal of Stalin? After all, it was through their allegiance to Stalin that all of these men had come to power. How could they attack Stalin without calling their own legitimacy into question? The Presidium recognised the need for change but was afraid to move too fast, for fear that reforms adopted in an atmosphere of crisis might snowball and get out of hand by raising popular expectations, and thus create a crisis of even greater proportions. The Presidium thought that a cautious criticism of Stalin would head off ferment among both administrative personnel (afraid that they might be attacked or lose their jobs in any reforms of the old system) and the general population (who might clamour for more radical changes). The regime was probably correct to be afraid. After Khrushchev's Secret Speech in 1956 unrest broke out in Poland and Hungary; 1953 itself saw a rising of workers in East Berlin following Stalin's death. Perhaps in recognition of the danger the Soviet leadership in 1953 actually tried to press the other East European regimes to introduce modest reforms themselves. These regimes by and large resisted, which led to the explosions of 1956.

The next major step in de-Stalinisation came in 1955, when the Central Committee set up a commission to investigate Stalin's crimes. The commission's mandate was strictly limited. It was to condemn alleged 'abuses of power' that temporarily engulfed an otherwise 'healthy' Party – but it was to justify as necessary the measures that had been taken against the 'internal and external enemies of Lenin's party' at a time when the new 'socialist system' was being created. In other words, it was to justify Stalin's repression and the elimination of the different Bolshevik oppositions to his rule in the 1920s and 1930s. Stalin was considered to have been correct in liquidating the Trotskyist and Bukharinist oppositions of the 1920s. Similarly, collectivisation was to be defended, despite the brutalities meted out to the peasantry and the economic catastrophe to which it led. What, then, could the commission criticise? It attacked acts committed against so-called dedicated Party workers, as well as against innocent scientists, writers and other intellectuals. Nothing more [52: 67].

The commission was headed by a Party historian and ideologist, P. N. Pospelov, himself a Stalinist who, according to Roy and Zhores Medvedev in their book on Khrushchev, had engaged in many acts of mass repression in the 1930s, and had been editor of *Pravda*, the Communist Part newspaper, in the years before Stalin died [52: 68]. The commission's report was understandably moderate and cautious, but it could not conceal how Stalin had settled accounts with Party leaders at all ranks of the Party and state machine. Even such a cautious report had, in the words of the Medvedev brothers, a 'staggering effect', and the Presidium resolved to level a modest criticism of Stalin at the Twentieth Party Congress scheduled for February 1956. This was to be a general, unfocused criticism, but Khrushchev seized the opportunity and decided to push the Presidium into allowing him to redraft Pospelov's words and present them to the Congress as his Central Committee Report [34: *346–51*]. This was his now-famous 'Secret Speech'.

3   De-Stalinisation

The Secret Speech and Its Aftermath

Khrushchev delivered his famous denunciation of Stalin and the so-called 'cult of personality' at a closed session of the Twentieth Party Congress in February 1956. According to Roy Medvedev's account [50: *87–8*]:

> They [the delegates] listened in shocked silence, only occasionally interrupting the speaker with exclamations of amazement and indignation. Khrushchev spoke of the illegal mass repressions sanctioned by Stalin; of the cruel tortures to which many prisoners, even members of the Politburo, had been subjected; of the letters they had written and statements they had made before they died. He told of the conflict between Lenin and Stalin in the last months of Lenin's life and of Lenin's proposal that Stalin be removed from the post of General Secretary of the Party. He mentioned the dubious circumstances surrounding the murder of Kirov in 1934 and hinted broadly at the possible involvement of Stalin. He spoke of Stalin's confusion in the early days of the Second World War and his desertion of his post at that time. It was at Stalin's door that he laid the lion's share of the blame for the severe defeats of the Red Army at the start of the war and for the occupation of huge tracts of Soviet territory. According to Khrushchev, Stalin was the initiator of the mass repressions of the post-war period. He had destroyed over two-thirds of the members of the Central Committee elected at the Party's Seventeenth Congress in 1934 and in his last years was preparing for a fresh series of repressive measures, having already practically excluded Molotov, Mikoyan, Kaganovich and Voroshilov from participation in the leadership. Khrushchev declared Stalin to be principally responsible for the deplorable state of Soviet agriculture and for many gross mistakes in his direction of the Soviet Union's foreign policy. He told of how

17

Stalin had encouraged the flowering of the cult of his own personality, falsified the Party's history and even amended his own biography to reveal himself in a better light.

For all the sensation the details of the speech caused, far more important were its limitations and repercussions. As we have noted, the pressures leading up to some sort of criticism of Stalin had been building up since Stalin's death. Following Beria's removal relatives of camp inmates had been petitioning for the release of prisoners, and several thousand had by 1955 been let go and rehabilitated. The Pospelov Commission had found itself unable totally to bypass the unavoidable issue of Stalin's methods of rule. Finally, the economic crisis had not improved, and so a more open policy of de-Stalinisation was necessary to improve the morale of the general population. Nevertheless, as one can imagine, any attack on Stalin and the way he had ruled would inevitably threaten many people who had won power and privileges under this system, not least Khrushchev himself. Therefore Khrushchev's speech was severely limited in what it was prepared to reveal. To begin with, the very act of making the speech was itself a compromise – a risky and perhaps astounding compromise, but a compromise nonetheless. According to Khrushchev's memoirs, Stalin's closest former associates – Voroshilov, Molotov and Kaganovich (surprisingly, he does not include Malenkov in this group) – feared reprisals over their past role and forcefully opposed any reference to Stalin's 'crimes'. Others, such as Malenkov, who had also played a central role in the repressions and also had a great deal to fear, apparently resisted the idea less vigorously. In the end Khrushchev won the day by indirect threats. The millions of prisoners in the camps were going to be released whether the leadership liked it or not, and soon the whole world would know of the terror. It was, he argued to his colleagues, better for the leadership to come clean now than to risk public outrage later on. Even this argument did not prevail. Finally, Khrushchev said he would use his right as Party First Secretary to address the congress with a personal statement. Only then, when faced with the prospect of a *fait accompli*, did the other Presidium members give in. And so it was agreed that a speech would be made, but that it should be delivered at a closed session of the Congress, and not in public [34: *346–51*]. This was done in dramatic fashion, as Khrushchev waited until the Congress had ended and then issued a call for delegates to return from their hotels for an emergency session. When they had

18

arrived the doors were closed and Khrushchev himself chaired the session. The only order of business was the speech, in which he denounced a number of Stalin's 'crimes' and abuses of power, mainly the elimination of old Communists (almost all of only secondary importance) and innocent intellectuals [34: Appendix 4].

Secondly, the contents of the speech were also a compromise. The speech talked of crimes, but began only with the events following the assassination of Sergei Kirov in December 1934. Kirov had been head of the Leningrad Communist Party and was seen by many (probably incorrectly) as a possible rival to Stalin. His murder, which Stalin almost certainly ordered, was used as a pretext to launch the wave of repression which culminated in the Great Purges of 1936–1938. By dating his criticism of Stalin from this time, Khrushchev tacitly accepted the repression of various opposition movements against Stalin during the 1920s, the most important being the Left Opposition of Trotsky, the Joint Opposition of Trotsky, Zinoviev, and Kamenev, and later the Right Opposition of Bukharin, Rykov, and Tomskii. However, other, minor oppositions had cropped up even within the Central Committee in the early 1930s, and their leaders, too, were severely dealt with, being expelled from the Party and exiled to far away parts of the USSR [79]. These actions, too, found no place in Khrushchev's speech. Nor did the speech question the brutalities of forced collectivisation, when millions of peasants were uprooted from their land and forcibly deported, many of them dying *en route* to labour camps [9]. There was equally no mention of the hardships and repressions faced by the urban population during industrialisation, of the famine of winter 1932–1933 when from 5 to 8 million people lost their lives, or of the show trials of 1929–1931, when a number of totally fictitious opposition movements were invented and many innocent people in the industrial and economic-planning administrations were persecuted, including through the use of torture [51: *240–4, 258–84*; 18: *91–6*]. As the Medvedev brothers point out (and as Roy Medvedev has described so chillingly in his book on the Stalin era, *Let History Judge*), the reign of terror had begun long before 1934, yet Khrushchev said not a word about this.

Even regarding the period after 1934 the speech was not totally honest. It dealt only with 'crimes' against top-ranking officials, and not with the repression and terror of ordinary citizens. Isaac Deutscher, in an article written just after the contents of the speech became known in the West, went even further and attacked

19

Khrushchev for bringing to light the persecution of only relatively insignificant members of Stalin's inner circle – people who had become top officials only because Stalin had eliminated the core of both leaders and rank-and-file veterans of the 1917 Revolution. There was no mention of the purges of the original Bolshevik leadership, many of whom had lived and worked in exile with Lenin, had played leading roles in the 1917 Revolution, and formed the backbone of the Party and government apparatus in the 1920s (including large numbers who, to their later cost, had supported Stalin in his rise to power, only to be killed in the Purges) [16: *11*]. Such omission was for good reason: Khrushchev and all those who had come to power through Stalin had done so because Stalin had won the power struggles of the 1920s and eliminated the old Bolsheviks of the revolutionary period. What would it say about the right of Khrushchev and his associates to rule the country if Stalin's old opponents were to be rehabilitated and their case against Stalin acknowledged as correct? This is why the critique of Stalin was of *Stalin the person* and not of *the Stalinist system*. This is also why the critique dealt with events that took place only after Stalin and his system were firmly in control. The monarch had to be discredited, but without discrediting the line of succession.

The Secret Speech did not remain 'secret' for long, and in fact was not intended to. It was, on Party orders, read out at local Party and workplace meetings. It was soon published abroad the world over. The speech had its enemies, primarily the old guard who felt threatened by it (Voroshilov, Kaganovich, Molotov, Malenkov and others of Stalin's former companions) and the 'mini-Stalins' in Eastern Europe (Bierut in Poland, Rakosi in Hungary, Novotny in Czechoslovakia). But the overall reaction inside the Soviet Union was one of enormous approval, all the more so as it was accompanied within a few months by the release of some 8 to 9 million political prisoners from the labour camps, compared to just 12,000 who had been set free prior to the Twentieth Congress. Yet the reaction, according to the Medvedev brothers, was so intense that it forced Khrushchev to put the brakes on the pace of de-Stalinisation. In June 1956 Khrushchev began a cautious retreat, giving Stalin credit for his 'services' to the Party and the revolutionary movement and toning down the scale of Stalin's alleged abuses of power [52: *19–20, 70–4*]. The cultural thaw which had begun soon after Stalin's death was also ended, as described in the next section.

The retreat led directly to a moratorium on any further probes into the past and on further denunciations of crimes and their perpetrators. This moratorium precluded any consideration of rehabilitating active opponents of Stalin convicted at the open Purge trials of 1936–1938, most notably Bukharin, Zinoviev, Kamenev, Rykov, Rakovsky and Pyatakov. Similarly, there was to be no review of the repressions carried out during collectivisation or the show trials of 1929–1931. Needless to say, this completely precluded any review of the so-called 'Trotsky question' and the political merits of Trotsky's case against Stalin. In the words of the Medvedev brothers, 'Khrushchev and his colleagues were reluctant to undermine the foundations of their own power, power which had been gained under the old system' [52: 73–4].

Despite this caution the average Soviet citizen still considered Khrushchev favourably: Khrushchev received credit both for attacking Stalin and for those small improvements that had taken place in the urban and rural standard of living. From the point of view of the old-line leadership, however, some of the 'damage' caused by the speech was irreversible, Khrushchev's back-pedalling notwithstanding. As we discuss in the next section, Khrushchev's revelations sparked popular outbreaks in Poland and Hungary, the latter ending in a Soviet invasion of the country [39]. Domestically, the mass rehabilitation of prisoners, according to the Medvedevs, threw serious doubts on Communist Party ideology: in the face of all these revelations, how could the Party be the bastion of 'socialist democracy' that it had claimed and that Party loyalists had believed it to be [52: 72–3]?

Limitations of De-Stalinisation at Home and Abroad

In many ways the apex of de-Stalinisation came in 1961, at the Twenty-Second Party Congress, where Khrushchev delivered an even more direct – and this time open – condemnation of Stalin, including attacks on Stalin for unpreparedness and ineptness during World War II. Stalin's body was removed from Lenin's mausoleum in Red Square and placed in a grave by the Kremlin wall, which was then covered with concrete to ensure that it could never be removed in the future [50: 208–11]. Eye-witness accounts of the time indicate that this Congress led to real ferment among the Soviet population.

When Stalin's body was taken out of the mausoleum Red Square was packed with people openly debating and speculating about the future. Rumours of rehabilitations of old Bolsheviks, including Bukharin (but not including Trotsky) abounded. Yet these hopes were also disappointed. The rumoured rehabilitations did not take place, and in 1963 there was once again a tightening up. Stalin's name was partly rehabilitated and censorship became more strict.

To understand these vacillations it is necessary to look at the fate of Khrushchev's various economic and political reforms (described in detail in following chapters), as well as some of the failures of his foreign policy. His agricultural reforms in particular had run into a dead end. Living standards were starting to fall, and soon after the Congress, in early 1962, he was to impose price rises which would provoke strikes and demonstrations. Faced with this situation, Khrushchev had come to opt for what seemed to be more and more arbitrary reorganisations of decision-making and executive structures, including the Communist Party itself. These proved to be no more than tinkering with the system, and so they, too, failed to improve the situation. They did, however, increasingly alienate the national and local Party leaders, on whom Khrushchev's hold over power depended.

It is against this background that the Twenty-Second Congress took place. It had been called not to denounce Stalin, but to ratify a new Party programme, in which Khrushchev impetuously and demagogically declared that the Soviet Union had already constructed socialism and would advance to 'full communism' by the year 1980. The Medvedevs persuasively argue that both the new programme and the attack on Stalin were in large part a response by Khrushchev to his growing unpopularity and the population's impatience with the country's economic difficulties, and an attempt to revive his waning reputation [52: *146–51*]. But it was also more than that. De-Stalinisation had always been for Khrushchev a vehicle for weakening or removing possible political rivals whom he would attack as defenders of the old guard. The Twenty-Second Congress was no exception [80: *141–75*]. Here, too, Khrushchev's efforts were far from successful.

One of the more interesting features of this period was the way in which the fate of Khrushchev's foreign policy reinforced these domestic trends.

Stalin's death ushered in a number of major changes in Soviet

22

foreign policy. The new leadership moved rapidly to negotiate an end to the Korean War, followed by the gradual evolution of a new policy of 'peaceful coexistence' with the Western capitalist powers, primarily the United States [70: *612*; 50: *72–4*]. Yet the Khrushchev years remained ones of high tension, including several international crises which brought the Soviet Union and the United States to the verge of open conflict. We cannot give a detailed account of Khrushchev's foreign policy in so short a book. Instead, we shall emphasise those events which had the greatest impact on internal developments inside the USSR and the fate of de-Stalinisation.

The first main area of change was the Soviet Union's relations with Eastern Europe. In early 1954 Khrushchev initiated moves to build a reconciliation between the USSR and Yugoslavia. Yugoslavia's Communist Party, led by Josip Broz Tito, had come to power following World War II on the strength of its leadership of the anti-Nazi partisans. It was thus the only East European Communist Party not to have been imposed by the Soviet Union's Red Army, a fact which had important repercussions for Yugoslavia's domestic and foreign policies. In 1948 Yugoslavia had broken with Stalin and declared itself non-aligned in the Cold War, and had come to assume a leading role in the so-called non-aligned movement. Domestically, although the Yugoslav League of Communists maintained for itself a monopoly of political power, it exercised far less centralised control over both politics and the economy. These two factors caused serious difficulties for Khrushchev's efforts to heal the split between the two countries. Khrushchev wanted Yugoslavia to integrate itself back into the military and economic alliance which the Soviet Union had built with the other Communist states of Eastern Europe, but this Yugoslavia refused to do. Moreover, Khrushchev constantly feared that Yugoslavia's more relaxed internal regime would lead the other countries of Eastern Europe to follow its lead and loosen their own economic and military ties with Moscow [73: *164–5*].

To some extent Khrushchev's fears were realised, although this probably had far less to do with Yugoslavia than with developments inside the Soviet Union following Stalin's death. We have already noted how Beria, and then Malenkov favoured an easing of the Soviet Union's heavy-handed control over Eastern Europe. In June 1953 the workers of East Berlin expressed their frustrations with Stalinist rule by staging an uprising, which had to be put down by Soviet tanks [61: *103*]. Yet far from entrenching the hard-liners inside the Kremlin, the event seems to have convinced Malenkov of the need to act quickly to ease the social tensions caused by the mini-Stalins still in power in Poland, Hungary, Czechoslovakia, and the other Communist regimes.

In Hungary, for instance, the new Soviet leadership – largely on the urging of Malenkov – had forced the old Stalinist ruler, Rakosi, to give up power in 1953; Moscow backed the reformist Imre Nagy. Yet Rakosi, with the support of conservatives in the Soviet leadership and probably the tacit approval of Khrushchev, proved stronger than expected and soon worked his way back into control over the Hungarian Communist Party and the government, putting many of his enemies in jail [73: *167–8*]. Following Khrushchev's secret speech attacking Stalin in early 1956, mass demonstrations in Hungary forced Rakosi from power, and Nagy became the new prime minister. Yet the popular movement wanted more than just changes in the Communist Party leadership. Demonstrations attacked the secret police, and workers throughout the country set up a network of workers' councils, which in many areas took over the job of local administration, including policing and transport. When Nagy, bowing to popular pressure, announced that Hungary would henceforth have a multiparty system, would become a neutral country, and would no longer take sides in the Cold War, Khrushchev, after some prevarication, gave in to demands from conservatives inside the Kremlin and invaded Hungary. Nagy was arrested and later executed, and a pro-Soviet regime led by Janos Kadar was put in his place [39; 73: *169–72*].

By contrast, popular demonstrations in Poland at the same time did not provoke a Soviet invasion, mainly because the demonstrators appeared content to accept fairly minor changes in the Polish Communist Party leadership, rather than sweeping reforms of the entire government structure. The Communist Party as an institution never appeared in danger of losing power, and there was no question of Poland leaving the Warsaw Pact [61: *219–21*].

As already mentioned, the invasion of Hungary had enormous repercussions for Soviet politics. It permanently set back the policy of introducing reforms in Eastern Europe [81]. Conservative Stalinist regimes were allowed to stay in office in countries like Czechoslovakia and Bulgaria because Moscow now saw them as less dangerous than the threat of popular uprisings in countries where reforms had been encouraged. It also severely weakened the standing of Communist

Parties in the West, many of whose members quit their parties in protest at the invasion. Insofar as Moscow traditionally relied on these Communist Parties to foster Soviet interests abroad, this was another blow to Soviet foreign policy. But most of all it contributed to the reaction inside the Soviet Union against de-Stalinisation. Quite simply, the old-line Stalinists still in the leadership (Molotov, Kaganovich, and their supporters) were able to say 'we told you so'. The cultural and political thaw, which had lasted from soon after Stalin's death until the aftermath of the Hungarian invasion, was momentarily reversed, a point we take up at the end of this section.

An event with equally profound implications was the USSR's almost total split with China. One issue in the dispute was the Chinese Communist Party's opposition to Khrushchev's attacks on Stalin, whom the Chinese leadership, in particular the Party leader Mao Tse-Tung, continued to extol as a great 'revolutionary'. This must at least partially have been caused by the Chinese leadership's opposition to any kind of internal liberalisation, such as Khrushchev appeared to be carrying out in the USSR. It made no difference to the Chinese that the results of this 'liberalisation' were actually quite modest. They obviously considered it a dangerous precedent. A second issue was Khrushchev's policy of 'peaceful coexistence' with the West (discussed below). The Chinese continued to advocate – at least in words – a policy of international revolution. Here, too, this had its roots in the practical needs of the Chinese leadership. They were at the time attempting to increase their influence among the newly-emerging third world nations, many of whom had won independence out of anti-colonial struggles and were deeply suspicious of continued Western domination, especially over their struggling economies. Finally, there was a less obvious basis to the Sino-Soviet split, namely the USSR's decreasing economic aid. From soon after Khrushchev came to power the Soviet Union began curtailing economic aid to China. It withdrew many of its technical advisors who had helped construct Soviet factories in China, and stopped sending spare parts for Soviet weapons and for Soviet machines, on which much of Chinese industry had come to depend. It is difficult to know whether this decline in economic aid was a Soviet response to the growing tensions between the two countries or whether it was a major cause of them. Whatever the case, relations between the two countries continued to deteriorate. Despite efforts by Khrushchev to forestall a split in 1960, in 1961 the Chinese walked out of the Twenty-Second Congress and attacked that Congress's criticisms of Stalin. Diplomatic and trade relations grew worse during the ensuing year, and by 1963 the rupture was total. In 1964 and 1965 there occurred a number of shooting incidents on the Soviet-Chinese border [61: *222–30*; 50: *143–4, 149–50, 155–6, 196–8*].

The Sino-Soviet split reverberated throughout the Communist world. It certainly weakened the potentional unity of the Communist movement in international affairs, and in this sense it was no doubt welcomed in the West. Although this would be difficult to prove, it probably also set certain limits on the conservative reaction *against* de-Stalinisation inside the Soviet Union and in Eastern Europe. We know from Westerners living in the Soviet Union at this time that the Chinese, by their defence of Stalin, made themselves deeply unpopular in the USSR. They thus eliminated any opportunity they might have had to influence Soviet and Eastern European politics, or the policies of the Western Communist Parties. The one exception was Albania, which all along supported the Chinese position on Soviet 'revisionism' and also broke with the Soviet Union.

Khrushchev's dealings with the United States also produced contradictory results. Khrushchev became famous for easing the Soviet Union's hostility to the United States and for advocating the doctrine of 'peaceful coexistence', according to which the two systems of capitalism and socialism would compete for influence in the world without resorting to direct armed conflict [61: *27–32*]. Yet both sides constantly pushed the limits of confrontation. When in 1960 the former Belgian colony of the Congo achieved independence and was led by a marxist-oriented leader named Patrice Lumumba, the United States openly encouraged a civil war in that country and its Central Intelligence Agency probably played a direct part in Lumumba's murder. In early 1961 the United States also supported an invasion of the island of Cuba, whose leader, Fidel Castro, had become a Soviet ally. The Soviet Union, in turn, continued to give certain limited support to anti-colonial movements and tried to bolster its influence among the newly-independent third world nations. In Europe tensions over the post-war division of Berlin also led to confrontation, culminating in the building of the Berlin Wall in 1961, which for 28 years divided Communist East Berlin from the Western half of the city, which was occupied by the three victorious Western Powers (the United States, Britain, and France) and was politically tied to the German Federal Republic [50: *180–4*; 61: *234–5*].

The Berlin crisis was not simply a case of great power rivalry. It marked a temporary setback for Khrushchev's efforts to win more resources for agriculture and light industry. Instead, the military and heavy industry were able to use the crisis (which they may, in fact, have helped provoke) to reverse previous cuts in defence spending and push Khrushchev into adopting a more bellicose stance in his dealings with the West [80: *170–5*]. This was to foretell even more serious consequences from the next major international crisis, the Cuban missile crisis of October 1962.

The long-term roots of the crisis lay in American military hostility towards Cuba, coupled with a US-led international economic embargo of the island. Khrushchev, giving in to demands from Castro to help him defend the island from possible US assault, installed nuclear missiles in Cuba. When the United States discovered this, President Kennedy imposed a full naval blockade on the island and threatened an invasion. For just over a week the world stood poised on the edge of an all-out nuclear war, until Khrushchev relented and withdrew the missiles in exchange for an American pledge to remove missiles from Turkey which threatened the South-West part of the Soviet Union [80: *261–76*].

Although the Cuban missile crisis led to improved relations between the superpowers, culminating in the 1963 treaty banning tests of atomic weapons in the atmosphere, its impact on Soviet domestic life was profound. Coming on top of his serious domestic difficulties, Khrushchev's lost gamble and the humiliation which the Soviet Union was seen to suffer seriously and irreparably weakened his political position. As with the first wave of de-Stalinisation following the Hungarian uprising of 1956, the second wave launched at the Twenty-Second Party Congress came to a sudden halt [30: *68–70*].

This is demonstrated quite clearly by looking at cultural policy under Khrushchev and his often turbulent relationship with the so-called creative intelligentsia. Stalin's death had been followed almost immediately by a cultural thaw. Largely under Malenkov's influence, censorship was relaxed, and writers began to take up previously taboo themes, such as bureaucratic corruption and abuse of power. They equally began to challenge the authority of the conservatives at the head of the Soviet Writers' Union. During this period the journal *Novyi Mir*, under its new editor Aleksandr Tvardovskii, played a prominent role, although Tvardovskii was temporarily removed in

27

1954 as Malenkov began to lose influence to Khrushchev, who up until then had shown no great liberal tendencies in cultural matters [29: *410–11*; 12; 59]. With the Twentieth Party Congress, however, the thaw gathered momentum – only to be cut short by the retreat from de-Stalinisation in the wake of the Hungarian rising [59: *95*]. Whatever his own inclinations, Khrushchev clearly responded to the pressure of those who believed that de-Stalinisation endangered the very foundations of the Soviet elite's power. The famous poet and novelist, Boris Pasternak, for example, was never allowed to print his novel *Doctor Zhivago*, which gave a critical portrait of the early years following the Bolshevik revolution. When, in 1957, Pasternak had the novel published in the West and a year later won the Nobel Prize for literature, Pasternak was expelled from the Soviet Writers' Union and was cruelly denounced in the press. As a result of this harassment his health deteriorated and he died in 1960 [50: *134–6*; 29: *411–12*].

More ominous were the events which followed the Cuban missile crisis. As Khrushchev had consolidated his political position and prepared the way for the new round of de-Stalinisation at the Twenty-Second Congress, the intellectual thaw was not only resumed, but in many areas proceeded with great dynamism. Perhaps the highlight of this period was the 1962 publication in *Novyi Mir* of Aleksandr Solzhenitsyn's shattering portrait of life in Stalin's labour camps, *One Day in the Life of Ivan Denisovich*. This was an extraordinarily radical event in the post-Stalin USSR, and both the book and Solzhenitsyn subsequently became world famous. Yet this period, too, came to a close with the new conservative offensive. Criticism of Stalin was curtailed. In early 1963 Khrushchev himself openly praised Stalin's 'services' to the Communist Party and the world Communist movement and warned against continued criticism of the dictator, just as during the retreat of 1956 [50: *220*]. Symptomatic of this turning point was an exhibition of contemporary Soviet art held in December 1962 at the Manezh gallery near Red Square. Conservatives in the leadership arranged to take Khrushchev to visit the exhibition, where they engineered a confrontation between him and a group of abstract painters whom they had secretly invited to display their works that very day. Khrushchev had an enormous row with some of the artists, accusing them of creating filth. The event was widely publicised, and the assault on artistic freedom had begun [12: *146–7*; 50: *216–18*; 80: *298–304*].

Although Khrushchev's personal tastes in art and literature were said to be conservative, this does not explain the clamp-down. He had little or no knowledge or appreciation of painting, but he read avidly and his literary tastes, though perhaps unsophisticated, were by no means philistine. He had openly championed many radical artists, including Solzhenitsyn, and attempted to maintain warm relations with them for a while following the Manezh incident [50: *219–20*]. Later, when he had been removed from office, he became quite friendly with some of those whom he had attacked. When Khrushchev died in 1971, he specified in his will that his grave was to be marked by a bust sculpted by Ernst Neizvestnyi, the artist with whom he had had the most heated argument at the Manezh [50: *259–60*]. No, the causes of the retreat were political: Khrushchev, who had launched the second wave of de-Stalinisation largely as a weapon against his rivals, was now on the defensive. The momentum was passing to the opponents of de-Stalinisation: both older Stalinists and new entrants into the political leadership who wanted to protect their newly-won position.

The cultural climate was to deteriorate further after Khrushchev's downfall: dissident writers were openly harassed, imprisoned, or, like Solzhenitsyn, forcibly expelled from the Soviet Union. Perhaps because of the ultra-conservatism of the Brezhnev years, the intellectuals tended to feel that Khrushchev, for all his faults, had nevertheless made one great contribution to Soviet life: he had attacked Stalin and ended the terror, and at least laid the groundwork for a more thoroughgoing de-Stalinisation at some point in the future. They were to wait more than 20 years: the repression would be relaxed only after Gorbachev came to power.

Yet for all its importance, the fate of the artists and intellectuals was merely symptomatic of the general limitations inherent in de-Stalinisation. Khrushchev wished to reform the system, but not to change its basic structure. Whenever the structure appeared threatened he pulled back – either on his own initiative or under pressure from other groups in the political leadership more sensitive to the preservation of their own privileges.

4   Political and Social Reforms

Following Stalin's death Khrushchev had built up his own power base through his position as First Secretary of the Communist Party. Like Stalin in the 1920s, Khrushchev used this position to appoint or promote local Party officials loyal to himself, in particular the secretaries of *oblast'* committees (*obkomy*) (see the List of Russian Terms, p. vi). These people became delegates to future Party Congresses and many were elected members of the Central Committee. They had been instrumental in giving Khrushchev the support he needed when challenged by the Party old guard [69: *56*].

The most critical such moment came in 1957 when Molotov, Malenkov, Kaganovich and Voroshilov tried to oust Khrushchev as Party Secretary. In part their opposition stemmed from their resentments at de-Stalinisation and the realisation, in the Medvedevs' words, that Khrushchev's power had come at the expense of their own. But they were equally if not more alarmed at Khrushchev's rash promises to overtake Western production of meat, milk and butter in just three or four years, a move they considered dangerously adventurous. The Presidium met and 'ousted' Khrushchev, who replied that only the full Central Committee could unseat him. The Presidium was prepared to arrest him, but in the meantime some Central Committee members in Moscow loyal to Khrushchev heard that something was afoot in the Kremlin and informally contacted other members of the Central Committee. Within a short while enough of them had arrived in Moscow to call a full meeting of the Central Committee, and they saved Khrushchev's job. The opponents became branded as the 'Anti-Party group' and they were in turn ousted from power. It was a striking testimony to the changes that de-Stalinisation had brought that they did not become victims of political repression. Malenkov was made manager of an electric power station in Central Asia, and Molotov was made ambassador to Mongolia [22: *129–40*; 52: *75–9*].

Khrushchev's various reforms aroused considerable resentment among lower levels of the old guard, that is, bureaucrats who had come into their jobs under Stalin and feared for the loss of their privileges if there were any major political shake-ups. Many of them were discontented with his various schemes to decentralise parts of the economic administration. This discontent increased when Khrushchev eliminated the so-called secret envelopes to top officials. These were cash bonuses paid in unmarked envelopes at the end of each month as additions to the salaries of leading bureaucrats (secretaries of *oblast'* committees, members of the All-Union and Republican Central Committees, editors of newspapers, etc.). He also did away with other perks, for example, cars and chauffeurs for assistant factory directors, directors of institutes, and heads of ministry departments. These moves were popular with the intelligentsia and the public at large, who saw them as steps towards greater social fairness and egalitarianism, but they provoked bitterness among the bureaucrats who lost some of their privileges [52: *83*].

Khrushchev further undermined his support among the bureaucracy in 1961, when the Twenty-Second Party Congress introduced so-called Rule 25, which limited the number of years Party officials could stay in office (and thereby enjoy the privileges these offices brought). We shall discuss this in more detail later on, in Chapter 7, but it is important to mention it here as part of Khrushchev's basic reforms.

Khrushchev also introduced important reforms in the legal system. The campaign of de-Stalinisation had championed the need to adopt so-called 'socialist legality', that is, the practice of following definite rules and legal procedures to protect the position of both ordinary citizens and public officials. These moves brought an end to the arbitrary arrests and imprisonments that had characterised Stalin's terror. No longer were people awakened by knocks on the door in the middle of the night and carted off to secret police headquarters for lengthy interrogations, often followed by summary trials and executions. A new criminal code of December 1958 overturned the whole basis of trials and convictions that had prevailed under Stalin: the secret police could not conduct trials; convictions now required evidence and witnesses – confessions (often extracted by torture) were no longer sufficient to condemn a victim; sentences could not be carried out without appeal. However, none of these reforms eliminated the very real repressive apparatus, including the now-reformed secret police, that dealt with dissidents and others considered threats to the Communist Party's monopoly of power.

What is more, Khrushchev was unwilling to go too far with legal reforms. He introduced the law on 'parasitism', which allowed people to be punished for being out of work. This later became a frequent means of harassing dissidents: first they were thrown out of their jobs and then they were prosecuted for being 'parasites'. Khrushchev also reintroduced the death penalty for serious economic crimes, after he had earlier abolished it for all crimes except treason. Both of these moves were actually opposed by a significant number of public prosecutors and judges who took the cause of legal reform and the creation of a law-based society seriously and saw them as partial throwbacks to the old system [29: *350–3*].

The reform of the legal system had followed a major shake-up of the secret police following the Beria affair, which we have already mentioned in Chapter 2. The MVD was broken up and the secret police was reconstituted as the KGB (Committee for State Security), which in turn was put under direct control of the Communist Party, to ensure that no individual could again use it as a base from which to attempt to seize personal power. Following the Twentieth Party Congress the KGB was itself purged, with many new heads of the KGB administration coming from the Communist Youth League (Komsomol). This purge had been necessitated by the mass release of political prisoners from the labour camps and their subsequent rehabilitation and integration back into civilian life. Too many of the ex-KGB officials had been responsible for sending these prisoners to camps, and they could not be retained in the secret police if the latter was to have any sort of legitimacy in the eyes of the general population. This reform brought its own problems with it, however. Khrushchev was a notoriously bad judge of character [7; 50: *ix*], and many of the new appointees turned out to be careerists of questionable honesty and ability [50: *133*]. Perhaps more to the point, because the KGB still functioned as an agency to control the population and suppress internal dissent, it never enjoyed the public respect which the reform was intended to give it. Indeed, it could not so long as the system remained politically authoritarian. Thus for all the significance of the legal reforms, individual freedoms still remained limited. Social control through terror was replaced by more subtle forms of repression: loss of Party membership, denial of promotion, or being fired from one's job.

The Khrushchev period also saw some major social reforms. Khrushchev vastly improved social security benefits and raised the level of pensions, which under Stalin had been derisorily low: 10

rubles a month, when the monthly income needed to keep out of dire poverty was at least 30 rubles. Under Khrushchev pensions went up, to just about the poverty line. Thus pensions were not high, but at least with careful management and some good fortune the elderly could just about survive on them [40: *146–7*].

Under Khrushchev real wages also went up, especially those of agricultural workers. Most of this was accomplished by transforming a large number of collective farms (*kolkhozy*) into state farms (*sovkhozy*). Collective farms were nominally independent entities, whose workers (*kolkhozniki*) were not state employees, but members of the collective. Thus their incomes depended solely on what they received for the number of 'labour days' they put into the farm each year, plus whatever meagre profits were distributed by the farm after the harvest had been delivered or what they could earn on their small private plots. The standard of living on the collective farms was appallingly low, largely thanks to the practice under Stalin of charging the farms excessively high prices for the machinery they used and paying them very little for their harvests. In general it cost peasants more to grow food or raise livestock than they received from the state as payment. Although peasants were allowed to keep private plots for their own subsistence, these were subject to so many restrictions and confiscatory taxes that the average peasant earned less than half of a poverty-line income in 1954. State farm members (*sovkhozniki*) by contrast were state employees, were paid a regular wage, and were entitled to annual holidays, sickness benefits, pensions, and perhaps equally important, an internal passport, which under Stalin had been denied to *kolkhozniki* as a way of limiting their migration into the towns where job prospects and wages were far better than in the countryside. Thus by turning a significant number of collective farms into state farms the regime immediately raised the wages and general living standards of millions of rural workers and their families [40: *146–7*; 62: *213, 219*; 52: *24–30*; 57: *567*].

The government also made massive efforts to tackle the chronic housing shortage. The Bolsheviks had already inherited a terrible housing crisis when they took power in 1917, and the country had been too poor to make major inroads into it during the New Economic Policy (NEP) of the 1920s. Under Stalin housing was further neglected: millions of new workers flocked to the towns, but the government considered house-building of only minor importance compared to the investment needs of its industrialisation programme and starved it of resources. During World War II housing became worse still given the terrible destruction wreaked upon the European areas of the USSR. Khrushchev launched a truly massive campaign of housing construction to try to remedy the crisis. Millions of new housing units were thrown up in a short time. They were hastily constructed out of prefabricated and often poor quality materials, and their design was monotonous. The quality of construction work has always been notoriously bad in the USSR and this period was no exception. Units were built and declared ready for tenants when in fact they were still unfinished or actually unsafe. The public even coined a new expression: 'Khrushchev slums', or *khrushchoby*, a play on Khrushchev's name and the Russian word for slum (*trushchoba*). But these problems should not mislead anyone into thinking that the building programme was not a major contribution towards reversing nearly three decades of Stalinist neglect [21: *50–2*]. To put the difficulties into international perspective, anyone who has seen Moss Side in Manchester, Easterhouse in Glasgow, or similar projects throughout Great Britain will legitimately wonder if British architects, builders and politicians of the 1960s had not been favourably impressed by Khrushchev's building methods.

One of Khrushchev's major campaigns was his drive to reform the educational system. Under Stalin there had been a decided move away from the principle of polytechnical education favoured by the Bolsheviks in the 1920s, whereby children were exposed to a mix of academic and vocational learning, including principles of planning and job design. Stalin replaced this with a heavy emphasis on sterile, rote learning involving a great deal of memorisation and discouraging independent thinking [26; 27: *144–57*]. At the end of the 1930s Stalin also imposed fees for the final years of secondary schooling and all of higher education. Given the shortage of trained specialists and the fact that most people left school after three of four years at secondary level to take up a job, the ability to complete one's secondary education was at this time virtually a guarantee of admission into higher education, and with it the privileges that came with intelligentsia jobs (engineers, other types of technical specialists, higher-ranking administrators, scientists, writers, etc. – see the List of Russian Terms, p. vi). The fees system obviously gave many intelligentsia families privileged access to this escalator of social mobility – although for such low-waged intelligentsia occupations as teachers personal contacts were more important.

One of the first moves Khrushchev made was, therefore, to abolish school and college fees. But he also wanted to go further and attack what he saw as the anti-egalitarian attitude of the intelligentsia towards education and raise the prestige of working class occupations. This was combined with an attempt to re-introduce polytechnical education as a main part of the school curriculum. The years 1955–1957 saw a number of experiments in this direction, with many schools, especially in rural areas, allegedly enjoying some success at integrating work into the curriculum. However, a shortage of trained teachers put limits on how far these experiments could be extended 50: 128–30].

At the same time there was a pressing need to overhaul the existing system of vocational training, which was still based on the Labour Reserve Schools set up in 1940, when Stalin introduced universal labour service for adolescents. In March 1955 the schools had become voluntary, but they still provided industry, construction, and transport with some half a million new workers a year. The problem was that the training they offered was extremely poor, even by Soviet standards. Students were taught on outdated equipment and there was often no connection between the trades they were trained for and those which enterprises actually needed. The instructors themselves were badly trained. As a result enterprises usually found that they had completely to retrain Labour Reserve graduates from scratch, and eventually became reluctant to take these people on, considering it easier and more economical to train new workers themselves whom they hired directly at the factory gates [21: 72–4]. This was the background to Khrushchev's memorandum of July 1958, 'On Strengthening the Link Between School and Life and Further Developing the System of Public Education'. The memorandum attacked the elitism of the intelligentsia and top Party and government people, and the general aversion of them and their children to taking up working-class jobs. Khrushchev called for a re-emphasis on vocational training and – more importantly – the elevation of the prestige of manual jobs in both industry and agriculture.

Khrushchev's detailed schemes for reform called for an extra year of schooling in the middle years with a strong vocational content, the idea being to enable children to leave school both with a trade and with a basis for making an intelligent choice of career. This, as Roy Medvedev notes, was not really a re-emphasis on *polytechnical* (that is, all-sided) education, but a stress on vocational training, that is, training for a particular skill. In fact, the reform, if carried through as Khrushchev originally proposed it, would have meant a sharp curtailment of general and polytechnical secondary schools in favour of vocational schools [50: *130–1*].

The actual reform of November 1958 was not so impetuous and preserved the general secondary schools as the country's main educational institutions. Training in production was to take up one-third of the timetable in the ninth, tenth and eleventh grades (the final three years in the Soviet system), and children were to spend a specified number of months actually going into factories to be trained in industrial trades. The other side of the reform affected higher education, as Khrushchev adopted a number of measures to make it easier for working-class children to enter university, technical institutes or other institutes of higher education. Greater emphasis was now put on correspondence or evening courses, so that people holding full-time jobs could study for degrees. Khrushchev also set up so-called special sections, which were remedial programmes for workers with a certain amount of industrial experience through which they could improve their educational skills in preparation for later entry into higher education. Heads of higher education institutions were also pressed to accept a larger quota of working class children. This aspect of the reform had noticeable results, as the share of working-class students in higher education rose, thanks mainly to the vast increase in the proportion of evening or correspondence students in the total college population [48: *288–96*].

Khrushchev's educational reform met opposition on three grounds. First, factory managers opposed the secondary school reform because they rightly claimed that factories were ill-equipped to handle the influx of large numbers of pupils. School students, they argued, ought to be receiving vocational training in specially-constructed training institutions, with proper instructors, and not on the factory floor, where the pupils tended to get in the way of both shop floor supervisors and the skilled production workers who were supposed to train them (and who had enough to do just to meet their production quotas) [52: *144*; 21: *73–4*]. Second, intelligentsia parents opposed both aspects of the reform because they prejudiced their children's privileged access to higher education, and with it the ability of their children to enter privileged intelligentsia jobs. Finally, heads of higher education establishments complained that the emphasis on working-class recruitment was lowering 'academic standards'. The groups raising objections to the reform were sufficiently powerful to ensure that virtually every aspect of it was rolled back as soon as Khrushchev was ousted from power. The vocational training scheme was stopped. Instead the regime concentrated on developing a more traditional, three-pronged system of secondary education, whereby over the last 25 years the overwhelming majority of Soviet school children now earn a complete general secondary education, either in a general secondary school, or by leaving school after grade eight and going on to either a vocational training institute (PTU in Russian), or to a technical college (*tekhnikum*) for training as technicians or for low-level non-manual skilled jobs. At the same time the share of evening and correspondence students in the total tertiary population has dropped sharply. Of Khrushchev's changes, only the special sections for young adults with work experience survived [48: *267–74, 288–96*].

The educational reform is a good illustration of the combination of factors that helped subvert even the most well-intentioned of Khrushchev's campaigns. The reform was ill-thought out and hastily implemented, so that no time was allowed to build and equip the necessary vocational training institutions or to train the required instructors. At the same time the egalitarian aspects of the reform threatened the privileged position of the intelligentsia, who immediately perceived that it posed a threat to their group interests and vigorously opposed it. The opposition of university rectors and other heads of tertiary institutions about falling standards was in large part a reflection of this elitism on the part of the intelligentsia.

5   Agriculture

Agriculture has always been the weak link in the Soviet economy. Collectivisation had been designed to place agriculture on a modern, mechanised footing, thereby providing both a pool of potential labourers for work in industry and construction, and an increased supply of food and agricultural raw materials. In reality, the brutal methods by which collectivisation was enforced and the widespread peasant resistance which these provoked led to a sharp fall in livestock herds and agricultural produce, as peasants slaughtered their animals and burned their grain rather than give it over to the new collective farms which they did not want to enter. The result was a drastic decline in the standard of living. The low point of this process was the famine of winter 1932–1933, already referred to above.

Stalinist policy, from the 1930s until his death in 1953, was to treat the agrarian sector as nothing more than a limitless source of exploitation [52: *24–31*; 76: *95–6*]. The vast majority of peasants were not state employees, but members of collective farms (*kolkhozy*). These, as we have already mentioned, were nominally independent bodies that had contractual arrangements with the state. Each farm had a quota of produce – grain, dairy products, meat, etc. – which it had to sell to the state at prices which the state itself set. In addition, until the mid-1950s, the *kolkhozy* did not own or operate their own agricultural machinery, but leased the use of equipment from state-run Machine-Tractor Stations (MTS), whose workers were state employees. The MTS were paid in kind, that is, with produce from the farms, in return for their services. In theory, after the *kolkhoz's* compulsory sales to the state and its payments in kind to the MTS, there should have been a surplus. This, where it existed, was distributed to the individual *kolkhozniki* according to the number of 'labour-days' (*trudoden'*) each had put in over the course of the year. If after this there was still something left, the *kolkhoz* could sell it in the towns at state-determined prices and distribute the money to its members. In addition, peasants were allowed to keep small private plots, including limited numbers of livestock, on which they could grow vegetables or produce meat or dairy products.

In reality the system left the peasants constantly impoverished. The prices paid by the state for compulsory deliveries were so low that they did not even meet the costs of production. The payments in kind to the MTS were punitively high (the MTS system was designed as a way surreptitiously to pump extra resources out of the countryside into the state treasury). Surpluses were, therefore, rare. Worse still, if bad weather or poor management left a *kolkhoz* unable to meet its quotas – which were usually set unrealistically high – the deficit was carried over to the next year, so that the *kolkhoz* then had a double burden to make up: the current year's quota *plus* debts owed from the year before. Needless to say, the vast majority of *kolkhozy* fell progressively into debts from which they could not extract themselves. The normal response would have been for the peasants to flee the land. But to stop just this development, in the early 1930s the regime had introduced the system of internal passports, without which it was impossible to move to the towns. And *kolkhozniki* were not entitled to an internal passport. Only if their children declined to register with the *kolkhoz* and managed to enroll in a training course, higher education, or find a job in a town could they escape. But their parents were virtual prisoners on the land. The Medvedevs have accurately described the position of the peasantry under Stalin as 'semi-serfdom' [52: *31*].

After World War II the situation in the countryside worsened still further. Many able-bodied peasants had been killed; many able-bodied returning peasant soldiers did not go back to the land. The country was desperately short of food, yet Stalin refused to devote increased resources to agricultural investment; instead everything was poured into heavy industry and construction in an effort to speed up the post-war recovery. Thus the urban population was growing – and with it the demand for food – while the countryside was becoming less and less able to meet this demand. Stalin's response was to put heavier taxes on private plots, despite the fact that the plots had always provided a large share of the country's essential fruits and vegetables. The taxes were made so high that it was no longer profitable for peasants to cultivate them. They not only stopped working their plots, but destroyed what they had grown to avoid taxes. The theory had been that if the peasants were discouraged in this way from devoting time to their plots, they would work harder for the *kolkhoz* –

a policy Khrushchev was to attack in the 1940s and 1950s, only to resuscitate it himself later on [52: *29–31*].

Agriculture, therefore, suffered the dual problems of lack of resources and low motivation. The latter was perhaps a greater problem than the former, because it meant that the peasants neglected and misused what little equipment and resources they had. The problem of poor motivation remained the key stumbling block until the country's break-up, and is still a problem today.

According to the Medvedevs, in the late 1940s Khrushchev was the only one of the leadership around Stalin to have had any experience of rural life and to have understood at least some of agriculture's main problems, although even here his knowledge was superficial [52: *32*; 54: *161*]. In 1949 he managed to persuade the leadership to implement certain limited, but nonetheless major reforms. The main one was to push through the consolidation and amalgamation of small, unprofitable collective farms with larger, more prosperous ones, in order to create viable production units. Under his reform the number of collective farms was reduced by two-thirds, that is, to one-third their previous number. However, Khrushchev knew that this was nothing more than a holding action. Although it brought prompt improvements to the plight of the small and debt-ridden *kolkhozy*, unless the state changed its price and investment policies the rot would proceed to undermine the whole of the agrarian sector [52: *33–4*].

When Khrushchev became Party First Secretary in 1953, he immediately launched a major reform of the procurement system. In order to encourage peasants to produce more on their private plots, taxes and compulsory delivery quotas on produce from these plots were cut; peasants were given better pasture land and fodder for their livestock. To give peasants greater incentive to work harder on the collective farms, payments in kind – made to the peasants as payment for their work on the *kolkhoz* or as a share of end-of-year *kolkhoz* surpluses – were raised; pay per labour-day went up; and prices paid to *kolkhozy* and *sovkhozy* for deliveries to the state were also boosted, so that peasants would now have an incentive to raise overall production. The result was a rapid increase in *private* livestock herds, which, however, held back the expansion of herds kept by the *kolkhozy* and *sovkhozy*. In the state sector, the output of grain rose dramatically – by about 75 per cent – between 1953 and 1958. Khrushchev followed up these policies by converting large numbers of collective farms into state farms, already referred to above. This benefitted the poorer collective farms, which now found it easier to obtain credits, as well as the farm workers who now became state employees, were paid a regular (though relatively small) wage and became entitled to holidays, sick pay and pension benefits. Khrushchev also continued the policy of amalgamating smaller and poorer collective farms into larger, and hopefully more thriving ones. In all, the number of *kolkhozy* fell from 125,000 in 1950 to 69,100 in 1958 [52: *34–7*; 76: *103–4*; 63: *329–31, 336–8*]. Finally, Khrushchev tried to make the *kolkhozy* more efficient by reducing the influence of the Ministry of Agriculture in collective farm management and increasing Party control. This was consistent with Khrushchev's general approach to reform, which saw the Party – which was the base of his political support – as the avenue through which popular energies could be mobilised and channelled. To this end, in 1953 he put the Machine-Tractor Stations (MTS), rather than district offices of the Ministry of Agriculture, in charge of managing the collective farms, and made the local Party secretary head of each MTS [76: *100*].

These early planks of Khrushchev's agricultural policy brought results, as we have seen, but still left most of the underlying problems untouched. The new procurement prices, for example, were still below production costs for all but the most efficient farms, which continued to be starved of resources to invest in improvements and modernisation [54: *165–7*]. At a deeper level, these early policies were never intended as a long-term solution, which required massive new investment and a radical improvement in workforce morale. To meet these problems Khrushchev launched a number of campaigns and institutional reforms which failed, largely because of the combination of factors outlined in the Introduction. An examination of these is, therefore, valuable both as an account of the problems of Soviet agriculture in these years and as an illustration of the more general problems besetting Khrushchev's rule.

The Virgin Lands and Maize Campaigns

Khrushchev's successors and Western observers alike have traditionally blamed his agricultural failures on his tendency either to come up with 'hare-brained' schemes or to undermine basically sound policies by implementing them too quickly and without proper planning or

41

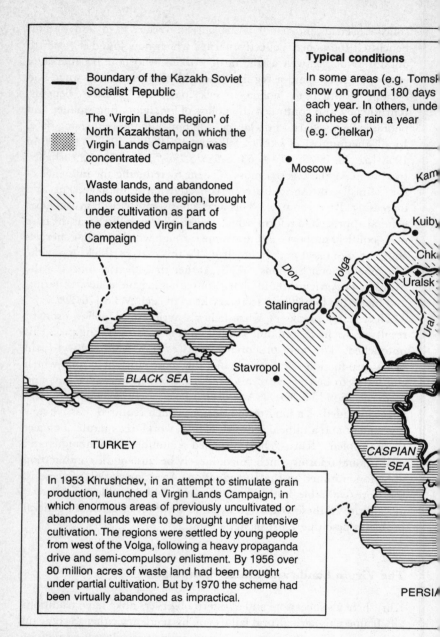

Legend:

— Boundary of the Kazakh Soviet Socialist Republic

The 'Virgin Lands Region' of North Kazakhstan, on which the Virgin Lands Campaign was concentrated

Waste lands, and abandoned lands outside the region, brought under cultivation as part of the extended Virgin Lands Campaign

Typical conditions

In some areas (e.g. Tomsk snow on ground 180 days each year. In others, unde 8 inches of rain a year (e.g. Chelkar)

In 1953 Khrushchev, in an attempt to stimulate grain production, launched a Virgin Lands Campaign, in which enormous areas of previously uncultivated or abandoned lands were to be brought under intensive cultivation. The regions were settled by young people from west of the Volga, following a heavy propaganda drive and semi-compulsory enlistment. By 1956 over 80 million acres of waste land had been brought under partial cultivation. But by 1970 the scheme had been virtually abandoned as impractical.

Map labels: Moscow, Kam, Kuiby, Chk, Uralsk, Don, Volga, Ural, Stalingrad, Stavropol, BLACK SEA, TURKEY, CASPIAN SEA, PERSIA

Map 2   The Virgin Lands, 1953–1961

resources. The reality, as we shall see, was far more complex. One need not ascribe to the one-sided view of those like Tatu, who see Khrushchev as a beleaguered reformer constantly blocked by intransigent conservative interests [80] to appreciate that Khrushchev's approach to agriculture was both more rational and better thought-out than his rivals claimed [76; 25; 33]. It was only during the last four years of his rule that, seeing that his policies were floundering and failing to produce the results he had hoped for – and promised the Soviet people – he resorted to more impetuous and ill-planned schemes and reorganisations. According to Smith, for example, Khrushchev understood full well that only a substantial increase in agricultural investment in the long term would help restore the agricultural sector to health, but Khrushchev was unable to win the resources for his investment policies, which were opposed by entrenched interests in the bureaucracy who sought to keep heavy industry and defence as priority areas. As a result, policies that Khrushchev had adopted only as short-term, stop-gap measures became permanent policies, largely because Khrushchev had to make the best of a bad deal. The results were sometimes disastrous. This interpretation, while undoubtedly correct, must nonetheless be qualified. Khrushchev may have understood the need for new investment, but it was only from 1960 onwards that he tried to wrest greater investment resources from the Presidium. During the early years of his rule he sought to expand agricultural output without any major redistribution of resources from heavy industry or defence, relying more on raising popular morale, prodding the collective farms themselves to provide their own investment, improvements in production techniques, and bringing new lands under cultivation [4; 80]. Equally, if not more important, Khrushchev's failures were due as much to the structural backwardness of the Soviet economy, in particular its agricultural equipment and chemical industries, as they were to the political battles being fought out between different sections of the ruling elite.

In late 1953 Khrushchev proposed to open up to farming millions of hectares of uncultivated land in Central Asia and Western Siberia. These lands were risky to cultivate because of the poor climate in these areas, which left them subject to drought and wind storms; but as the land was virgin it was also highly fertile, and so could be relied on to produce substantial yields *for a short time*. Beginning in 1954, large areas of virgin land were ploughed up – nearly 42 million hectares between 1954 and 1960, although not all of this represented a gain in sown area: some 10 million hectares were either unsuitable for cultivation or were taken out of production in non-Virgin Land areas. This still represented a net gain to agriculture of 33 million hectares. After some disappointing results in 1955, there was a large grain harvest in 1956, over half of which came from Virgin Lands or idle lands that had been brought into use [43: *82–8*]. In some ways this was the worst thing that could have happened, because the good harvest, which was due mainly to unusually favourable weather conditions, created a false confidence among Khrushchev and the rest of the leadership that these lands could carry on producing high yields for some time to come. In fact, the results were extremely variable, as Table 5.1 shows:

Table 5.1   Grain Production in Virgin Lands, 1954–1964
(million tons)

	1954	1955	1956	1957	1958	1959	1960	1961	1962	1963	1964
USSR	85.6	103.7	125.0	102.6	134.7	119.5	125.5	130.8	140.2	107.5	152.1
Virgin & idle lands	37.6	27.9	63.5	38.4	58.6	54.9	58.7	50.6	55.9	38.0	66.4

Source: [43: *88*].

Thus the excellent harvest of 1956 was followed by a near disastrous harvest in 1957. And although the grain harvests on the Virgin Lands recovered in subsequent years, actual yields per hectare soon began to decline. The gross yields were only maintained because more and more new land was brought under cultivation, a practice that had very definite limits and which led to catastrophic results in 1963 with serious long-term consequences. Although 1964 – ironically, the year that Khrushchev was ousted – saw a sharp recovery, including in the Virgin Lands, the harvest of 1965 was again bad. More to the point, the rapid growth in the urban population meant that even the good harvests fell far below the country's growing demand for food, a demand which agriculture, given its structural backwardness, was simply unable to meet [76: *108*].

The initial successes of the Virgin Lands campaign, and the excellent all-round harvest of 1958 (helped largely by good weather),

45

encouraged the belief that Soviet agriculture was on the verge of a huge take-off in production. The new Seven-Year Plan adopted in 1959 called for unprecedented increases in agricultural production [43: *118*]. Here the Virgin Lands would play a key role: they would serve to raise grain yields for the moment while new investment in equipment and chemical fertilisers could be made in the traditional agricultural areas of Ukraine and the Black Earth regions, which would then be able to increase their own productivity substantially [52: *118*]. At the same time, Khrushchev intended that with the Virgin Lands producing more grain, the traditional grain-growing areas could devote more land to growing fodder crops – primarily maize – to expand livestock herds. In line with this, in 1957 Khrushchev promised to catch up with the United States in the production of meat, milk and butter – an impossible task, as it meant tripling meat production [52: *75*]. Thus the Virgin Lands campaign was intimately linked with other policies designed to increase fodder production and the size of livestock herds.

What went wrong? The relative successes of the campaign up to 1958 placed Khrushchev in an unexpectedly difficult political position. Khrushchev himself was well aware that the Virgin Lands could not sustain their fertility and yields without both inputs of new investment and the diversification of agriculture away from just grain-growing (which depleted the soil and left the land susceptible to wind erosion), to include animal husbandry for manure and the introduction of pasture and grass lands to rest the soil. The Virgin Lands were to remain an exclusively grain-producing area only temporarily, until the older agricultural regions of Ukraine and Central Russia could be modernised. However, such modernisation required substantial new investment in machinery and fertiliser. Greater use of fertilisers was a daunting task, since the Soviet chemical industry was weak and would itself require massive investment in order to provide the fertilisers that were needed. It was similar with agricultural equipment. The Soviet Union's agricultural machinery industry simply did not produce enough tractors, harvesters, mowers, and the like for *both* the older agrarian regions and the Virgin Lands. And since the Virgin Lands had priority, almost the whole of the country's output of farm machinery went there. Thus the Virgin Lands campaign, which was supposed to create a breathing space to allow for the modernisation of the older regions, actually became an *obstacle* to their development [54: *174–5*]. Clearly this vicious circle could be broken only with large-scale new investment in the chemical and agricultural equipment industries. From where were these resources to come? The Seven-Year Plan had set down ambitious goals, but said hardly a word about new investments [43: *118–22*]. Eventually Khrushchev tried to win greater investment for agriculture, but here he came up against competing industrial and defence interests, whose patrons in the leadership refused to allocate the investment that was needed [43: *123–32*]. The rate of new investment in agriculture slowed down, especially in such vital items as trucks, grain combines, cultivators and mowers – a development exacerbated by the abolition of the Machine-Tractor Stations, discussed below. Farms had to keep old equipment in service longer by patching it up, thus hurting efficiency [76: *105*]. Perhaps more importantly, throughout Khrushchev's reign there was a deep and on-going shortage of equipment in the Virgin Lands, where it was vitally needed. Khrushchev was then left with the problem of how to carry on with his policies when the investment resources were not forthcoming. Short-term expediencies became permanent policies.

One such policy was Khrushchev's campaign to expand the production of maize. The idea was hopelessly ill-conceived. The Soviet Union simply does not have significant areas where both soil and weather conditions combine to allow maize growing. The crop had low yields and in many areas simply did not ripen. Nevertheless, Khrushchev was convinced that maize was the answer to the Soviet Union's food problems and pursued his maize policy long after it had been shown to be ill-advised [52: *62–5, 123–8*]. The results were extremely damaging, since maize displaced more traditional crops which would have given better results [76: *106*]. The difficulties which hit the maize campaign led to other blunders, most notably the policy of reducing the amount of fallow land. In order to increase output of maize and grain, Khrushchev ordered that farms should drastically reduce the amount of meadow land left fallow [80: *214*]. To enforce this policy the agricultural machinery industry halted the manufacture of equipment used for maintaining and improving meadows. The result was that these areas became overgrown, weed infested or swampy. A full third of meadow land in the country was abandoned, causing hay production to fall. In some areas hay had to be imported from other regions to feed livestock. Thus this policy led to the opposite result from what was intended. Instead of increasing the supply of animal feed (fodder in the form of maize and grain), it sharply cut the supply of feed (hay), thereby making it harder to meet targets for expanding the supply of meat [52: *126, 164–6*; 43: *125–6*].

Both the maize and fallow-land campaigns, though fundamentally flawed, might have achieved some measure of success had there been adequate supplies of new equipment and fertilisers necessary to preserve soil fertility and conserve moisture, and supplies of weed killer to prevent weed infestation. None of these resources was available and the result was disaster [76: *106*]. To make up for the lack of proper resources, Khrushchev tried to advocate more frequent ploughing, which in turn required a new type of plough, designed by the agronomist T. S. Maltsev. However, production of the Maltsev ploughs was always inadequate and farms could not obtain them in the quantities they needed. Moreover, the new ploughs were not as effective at preventing weed infestation as traditional ploughs, and thus required leaving at least 20 per cent of land fallow. As Khrushchev's fallow land policies made this impossible, farmers rejected the new ploughs even where they were available. The end result was that the new ploughing regime led to soil erosion – precisely what it was supposed to prevent [43: *158–61*].

Finally, the problem was compounded by the policy of T. D. Lysenko, a charlatan geneticist who influenced both Stalin and Khrushchev [53]. In this particular case, Lysenko advocated a totally unsound policy of early sowing in the Virgin Lands, where soil conditions were unsuitable and the crop was likely to be lost due to erosion. The combined effect of all these factors – the improper conversion of meadow-land; the lack of weed killer; the non-availability of proper ploughs; and Lysenko's scientifically unwarranted advocacy of early sowing – culminated in catastrophe in 1963: In that year there was an early thaw and drought in the Virgin Lands. There was a disastrous harvest failure and, more importantly, the loss of millions of hectares due to wind erosion [43: *161–7*]. This was followed by more catastrophic wind storms in 1965. According to the Medvedevs, one of whom is a biochemist and geneticist, it will take from one to two centuries before the affected areas will be arable again [52: *121*]. Here, too, the drive to push up production without adequate preparatory measures took its toll. The dangers of wind erosion had been well known from the beginning of the Virgin Lands programme, but preventive measures were simply too costly to implement. Moreover, the continued cultivation of monoculture – grain – had also left the open steppe lands vulnerable to erosion. But this, too, had not been simply a political decision. The very nature of starting up farming in previously uncultivated regions, with no indigenous agricultural population, meant that the Virgin Lands campaign had had to rely on inexperienced recruits from the countryside, many of whom became disheartened by the primitive living and working conditions and left. But without experienced farmers it was difficult to introduce diversification [54: *191–3*]. Here was yet another instance where the Soviet Union's economic backwardness blocked the investment needed to make Khrushchev's policy a potential success – in this case the investment in 'human capital', that is, in housing, roads, schools, cultural facilities, and other infrastructure which might have encouraged people to become permanent settlers.

Although the harvest in the Virgin Lands recovered in 1964, and Western Siberia and Kazakhstan continued to provide much of the USSR's grain right up to the present day, the Virgin Lands did not prove the answer to the country's agricultural problems. The productivity of these lands was poor and they could not compensate for the major structural imbalances plaguing Soviet agriculture as a whole.

The Ryazan Fiasco

Khrushchev's promise to catch up with the United States in meat and milk production had led him to launch his maize campaign, which in turn contributed to the eventual disaster of the Virgin Lands. It also had other damaging consequences. The Soviet system was highly bureaucratic, which means that officials were always jockeying for position and manoeuvring to improve their career prospects. This was especially important in a country like the USSR, where private wealth was not inherited, but was attached to the job one had. It was the opposite of the capitalist system, where wealth and privilege by and large assure access to certain jobs (top bankers, directors of large corporations, stock brokers, etc.), which in turn allow the perpetuation of that wealth. In the Soviet Union privilege came through access to a high-ranking job; these privileges could be passed on to one's offspring only through indirect and imperfect channels, primarily by securing them privileged access to higher education, which then gave them easier entry to high-status occupations.

49

Because of this system, when a new policy was announced officials often tried to outdo each other and climb on the bandwagon, in order to court favour with those higher up and win promotion. This is what happened with Khrushchev's policy of trebling meat supplies. The goal was simply impossible to achieve, given the backwardness of the Soviet livestock sector. Nevertheless, an ambitious regional party leader in Ryazan *oblast'* named A. N. Larionov, claimed that he would double meat production in his region in 1959. Khrushchev was so impressed that he promised Larionov considerable support to achieve his task, as well as probable promotion if he succeeded. Other regions were encouraged to follow suit, although many in the hierarchy knew that Larionov's promise was bluff. Larionov and the Ryazan *oblast'* Party Committee fulfilled their quota, but only at great cost to the region's livestock industry. Basically, they slaughtered every cow in sight. It was impossible to meet their promise by marketing just those beef ready for slaughter. Young animals were killed prematurely. Worse still, they slaughtered their dairy herds. Even this was not enough: the Party Committee had to *buy* cattle from other *oblasti*. In other words, the whole campaign was a charade, but a charade with catastrophic results, for it decimated both the livestock and dairy herds of the *oblast'*. In the end Larionov was unmasked and eventually committed suicide [25: *33–42*; 52: *94–101*; 80: *128–32*].

The effect of the Ryazan fiasco went far beyond this one *oblast'*, however. The central authorities were determined that such a swindle should never happen again. And so, swinging to the opposite extreme, they imposed equally bureaucratic restrictions on how many livestock *kolkhozy* and *sovkhozy* could slaughter. Even unproductive animals now had to be kept, which led to a build-up of huge stocks of old and economically useless cattle that the farms had to feed. Within a few years such animals, which were actually a drain on *kolkhoz* resources, amounted on some farms to between 30 and 40 per cent of their herds! Statistics on the size of livestock herds were impressive, but were economic nonsense. Here is an example of how a bureaucratic attempt to cope with one type of abuse led to an equally costly result [52: *110–11*].

The Attack on the Private Plots, Food Shortages, and Civil Unrest

With the initial success of the Virgin Lands campaign in 1956 the government felt that it could cut back on its reliance on private plots. So it imposed restrictions on them. It limited the size of plots in both the countryside and the towns. The owners of private plots *in the towns* (where Khrushchev had earlier encouraged residents to start up plots as a means of augmenting their own, and the country's, food supplies) faced the further restriction that the government now prohibited them from purchasing grain to feed their livestock. In 1959 the restrictions on urban plots were extended by banning all private livestock in the towns. However, the amount of private livestock in rural areas continued to grow, since farm managers tended to ignore the 1956 restrictions.

As difficulties mounted in the state sector, the pressure on private plots intensified, since Khrushchev believed – as Stalin had believed before him – that the peasants were devoting too much time to their labour-intensive plots and not enough to the collective farms. Restrictions were intensified by local farm chairpersons, who abused existing regulations and coerced peasants into selling private livestock to the farms. Even this move was counter-productive, since the *kolkhozy* could not feed their larger herds. Yields of meat and milk per cow declined, and milk actually became scarce. At the same time the prices paid to peasants for meat, milk and other priority items were reduced, eventually to levels so low that the peasants lost money by boosting output. As under Stalin, it now cost the peasants more to feed their animals than the state paid them for animal products. Thus the situation that Khrushchev had attacked in 1949 and sought immediately to rectify as soon as he came into a position of power now reappeared under Khrushchev's guidance. Coupled with other agricultural failures, food supplies lagged behind the increased demand for food in the towns [52: *160–3*; 54: *194*; 76: *109*].

To meet this situation Khrushchev sharply raised food prices in 1962. The result was a wave of civil disturbances, as workers protested against the price rises. The most serious was at Novocherkassk, an industrial town near the Russian city of Rostov-on-Don, close to the Russia-Ukraine border. Tensions in the town had already been heightened by wage cuts imposed by management at the local

51

electrical locomotive factory. When the price rises on meat and dairy products were announced on 1 June there were mass street demonstrations and a virtual general strike. Strikers blocked the railway line in and out of town and quickly won support from workers in other factories. Eventually the crowd of demonstrators grew and massed outside Communist Party headquarters. The protestors also attempted to spread the strike to other towns, but were effectively cut-off by government troops. Commanders of the local militia and the local military garrison refused to fire on the crowds, and troops had to be called in from outside. It was they who, on the second day of the disturbances, fired into the crowd. Eyewitness accounts vary, but official documents claim that 22 demonstrators were killed and 39 wounded. The real figure could be much higher. The town was under martial law for several days and dozens of strike leaders were imprisoned. So sensitive was the massacre at Novocherkassk to the Soviet government that even under Gorbachev people who attempted to write about it were censored and harassed. Only in 1990 did the press begin openly to discuss it. Petr Siuda, a participant in the strike, who in 1988 had tried to publish his account of the disturbances, was mysteriously killed two years later [74; 2: *44–6*; 28: *10–14*].

The MTS Reform

As we have noted, early in his rule Khrushchev tried to increase Party control over local agricultural management by giving the Machine Tractor Stations greater powers over *kolkhoz* administration. Suddenly, in 1958, he reversed this policy and decided to abolish the MTS altogether, despite considerable internal opposition [8: *349*]. This might have been an appropriate policy – or at least not a disastrous one – if it had been carried out gradually with proper regard for the resources the *kolkhozy* would need to assume control over the MTS equipment, to use and maintain it properly, to store it, and to acquire necessary supplies of spare parts and fuel. Unfortunately, none of this was done [43: *112*].

To begin with the MTS reform was hastily carried out, without proper planning. For instance, too little account was taken of the differing circumstances of large and small or prosperous and marginal *kolkhozy*. Some could relatively easily take over responsibility for handling and maintaining the new equipment and for financing its

52

purchase, while others could not. Another difficulty was that, whereas initially it had been planned to *merge* the MTS with *kolkhozy*, this policy was abandoned and the *kolkhozy* were forced to *buy* the equipment. The purchase prices then set for this equipment were virtually twice their book value, that is, what the equipment was actually worth after allowing for wear and tear. What is more, *kolkhozy* had to pay the same price for old and new equipment. Prices of petrol, lubricants and spare parts were also doubled. To make matters worse, the policy of gradually implementing these changes was discarded and the plan was compressed into one year. By the end of 1958 some 80 per cent of *kolkhozy* had purchased MTS equipment; the other 20 per cent, which were in an economically weak position, were given credit to pay. By January 1959, 8000 MTS had been abandoned, and 345 remained; by the end of 1959 there were only 34 MTS. Finally, no account was taken of the need to lay on, or invest in, buildings to house the new machinery, to instal fuel storage facilities, and to build repair shops. *Kolkhozy* also now had to pay the wages of the machine operators [52: *85–9*; 76: *101–2*].

The results of the reform as it was actually implemented were highly damaging to Soviet agriculture [52: *90–3*; 54: *176–80*]: *Kolkhozy* had to spend so much on the MTS equipment that other vital investment projects had to be deferred, for example, new dairy facilities or modernising animal husbandry. Equally, there were not enough skilled machine operators or technicians. Since MTS employees now became members of the collective farms they lost their status as state employees, with the protection of wages, holidays, and sickness and pension benefits that came with this. They also lost their internal passports. As a result many of these skilled workers simply left agriculture and took up jobs in the towns. The regime tried to coax them back by reforming their pay, pension and holiday conditions, but this concession came too late, and few returned. The combination of the loss of mechanics and the absence of time or money to build up proper storage facilities caused equipment to fall into disrepair.

Problems with equipment did not stop here, however. The high prices the collective farms had to pay for the MTS equipment drove many of them bankrupt, so that they were unable to buy new agricultural machinery. Sales of agricultural machinery therefore fell sharply. According to the Medvedevs this fall-off in sales led to unsold equipment piling up in the agricultural machine-building factories, which responded by cutting back on the manufacture of farm equipment. We have already noted how new farm investment – and with it the basis for future growth – declined drastically during these years. The problem was not that the *kolkhozy* did not *need* new equipment – they needed it desperately, increasingly so as the old and run-down equipment acquired from the MTS wore out. However, they could not pay for this equipment, and this led to a severe shortage of machinery on the farms. Many mechanised jobs now had to be done by hand [52: *90–1*; 54: *179–80*].

This, however, is only part of the story. The MTS reform also had serious political repercussions for Khrushchev's reforms, which also helps to explain the cutback in the production of agricultural machinery. Those wings of the Soviet bureaucracy tied to heavy industry and defence, and which had always opposed increased resources going into agriculture (which would have come at their expense), used the MTS reform to argue that now, having acquired the MTS equipment, the collective farms no longer needed new machinery, and for *this* reason the agricultural equipment industry was *ordered* to cut back production [76: *105*]. Thus it was not simply falling sales that led to a reduction in this industry, but the power struggle in which Khrushchev lost the argument for increased investment in agriculture.

The combined effect of the financial pressures on the *kolkhozy* and Khrushchev's unsuccessful bid for more investment was a serious drop in the level of mechanisation on the *kolkhozy* [25: *169–70*]. Indeed, a number of agricultural machinery factories had actually been converted to other production [80: *215*].

Finally, no adequate provision had been made for repair stations. Repairs had to be done on the *kolkhozy* themselves, but three-quarters of them could not set up their own repair shops, and repairs were carried out haphazardly. To remedy the situation the government set up what it called technical service stations in selected areas. Attempts to recruit mechanics back from the towns also slightly increased their number. But by 1964, the year Khrushchev fell from power, these technical service stations could only meet one-half of the demand for necessary repairs [52: *92–3*].

The MTS reform, as can be seen, exacerbated the problems of the *kolkhozy* at a time when decisions taken in Moscow were also going against agriculture. We can illustrate the strain the reform placed on the *kolkhozy* by citing just one example: in order to buy four tyres for a particular type of tractor (the 'Belarus'), a farm had to sell 13 tons of wheat [52: *93*]!

Political Reorganisations

In line with his policy of transferring management of agriculture from the Ministry of Agriculture to local officials of the Communist Party, Khrushchev initiated a major reform of the Ministry's functions. It was stripped of many of its executive responsibilities in the fields of supply and finance and made to concentrate mainly on agricultural research [43: *114*]. In addition, Khrushchev had also argued that the decision-making apparatus in agriculture ought to be closer to the sector it commanded. He considered that the All-Union Ministry of Agriculture in Moscow and the Republican Ministries of Agriculture in the Republican capitals ought to be relocated in rural areas. Again, the reform may have had some justification (the Ministries were highly bureaucratic and inefficient), but the reform ran into difficulties on a number of fronts [52: *111–13*].

First, like other Khrushchev reforms it was badly prepared and hastily carried out. This was a problem because the Soviet Union's backward economy and poor infrastructure (roads, railways and communications) helped undermine the reform, yet no time had been allowed to overcome these difficulties. For example, the staff at the All-Union Ministry of Agriculture had to commute to work from their homes in Moscow some two to three hours each way over bad roads. To take another example, the telephone system could not integrate the Ministry's new telephones into the Moscow telephone network. When the Ministry of Agriculture of the USSR wished to phone up the Ukrainian Ministry of Agriculture it might take several hours to put the call through, and then the parties might not be able to hear each other!

Secondly, the reform aroused considerable resentment among Ministry staff, partly because of the problems just mentioned, but also because part of the reform stipulated that executive staff should also carry out some manual tasks alongside ordinary manual workers. Their annoyance at this measure, and at the reform in general, led to 1700 out of 2200 staff giving notice within a year. They were replaced by unqualified personnel, which further reduced the Ministry's already-poor efficiency.

Parallel with this reform Khrushchev also ordered the transfer of agricultural educational and research institutes to rural areas. Again, on paper this looked sensible, as most of these institutes were located in towns. But there was no plan drawn up for this and none of the necessary investments in new campuses and facilities were made. When plans were made there was no money to implement them, so that the institutes could not function. Meanwhile, the existing, and often well-equipped institutes, were barred from admitting new students as a means of forcing them to move. They were on the verge of dying when they were saved by Khrushchev's ouster [52: *113–16*].

There were other political reorganisations which affected agriculture, in particular the division of the Party into industrial and agricultural wings, but we shall discuss these in later chapters.

Summary

The dismal harvest of 1963 forced the Soviet government to do what before that had been unthinkable. It dipped into its gold reserves to buy grain and meat from the West. Otherwise the regime would simply have been unable to feed its population during the winter of 1964 [54: *195–6*]. This was the ultimate testimony to the failure of Khrushchev's agricultural policies. This failure had a number of causes. To some extent Khrushchev had based his policies on the assumption that agriculture would receive large-scale new investment, but he then proved not powerful enough to win the resources to carry these investments out. Thus the political rigidities and conservatism of the system helped to subvert Khrushchev's objectives. The Soviet bureaucracy was highly competitive, with each Ministry jealous to protect the resources under its jurisdiction and the privileges of its personnel. Each also had its strong defenders in the Communist Party and government machine. Khrushchev simply could not defeat the traditional power of the interests defending heavy industry and the defence sector.

Other aspects of his policy, however, failed because Khrushchev, being trained in the Soviet system, pushed through his policies bureaucratically and often with little foresight or planning. Khrushchev, when faced with difficulties, also turned necessities into virtues, as with the Virgin Lands and maize campaigns, which originally had been seen as only temporary measures.

56

Finally, the long-term neglect of agriculture under Stalin and the inherent weakness of the USSR's agricultural machinery and chemical industries posed serious economic obstacles to further progress.

We should not, however, overestimate Khrushchev's failures in agriculture. Even during the bad years average agricultural output still rose, but not nearly to the extent that had been expected or *was needed*. The fact was that both the urban population and disposable incomes (that is, the money in people's pockets) were growing *faster* than agriculture could meet their demand for food. This was partly because the poor quality of Soviet consumer goods meant that people, when they had more money, chose to buy extra food instead. It was also in part because many of Khrushchev's *social policies* benefitted the poorer sections of society, and the poor spend a higher share of their income on food than do the better off. But it was also due partly to the failure of Khrushchev's policies, in particular the increased pressure he put on the private plots and the peasants in general towards the end of his reign. Not only did the plots produce less food *for the towns*, but the restrictions on private plots meant that peasants could now grow less food *for themselves*: they, too, became consumers looking to buy food on the market. All of these factors meant that the demand for food went up faster than the country could grow it [76: *108–9*].

Khrushchev's solution was to make more bureaucratic adjustments, reorganising the ministries here, or reorganising the Communist Party there. But these measures failed because he could not solve the *essential* problems: improving peasant morale and incentives, and giving them better equipment and investment resources with which to work. The two had to go together to be effective. But Khrushchev's policies either harmed investment (the MTS reform) or he failed to win new investment from the planners; while the pressure he put on the peasants reduced their incentives to work. No amount of tampering with the administrative or Party machinery could solve *these* problems. In this sense Khrushchev's opponents in the leadership were correct when they argued that the issue was not more investment, but how the peasantry used the equipment they had. But here they were arguing less out of insight into the nature of the system over which they ruled – and from which they drew enormous privileges – than out of defence of their own narrow interests. Hence they, too, had no answer to agriculture's crisis, which has continued to the present day.

6   Industry

The System of Bureaucratic Planning

The Soviet Union at the beginning of the Khrushchev period was an industrial giant and a world superpower. Moreover, the economy continued to expand while Khrushchev was in power, so that in 1964, when he was ousted from office, its major industries were far more developed and modern than at the time of Stalin's death. Table 6.1 shows how major industries fared.

A closer look at the table will show that this was an economy of terrible imbalances. Khrushchev's Seven-Year Plan (1959–1965) had called for light industry and consumer goods to grow faster than heavy industry (iron and steel, engineering, fuel and chemicals), but the opposite took place. Consumer goods production remained backward, and, like agriculture, totally unable to meet the needs of the population. What is more, the quality of what was produced in both heavy and light industry continued to be very poor – sometimes so poor that the goods could not be used. Production was inordinately wasteful: much of the fuel, raw material and metal produced by industry was lost during transport, ruined during use, or over-consumed. Thus much of what industry manufactured made little or no contribution to the country's well-being, even though it counted in the statistics as 'growth' [21: *160–76*]. The reason for this lay in the Soviet Union's particular form of bureaucratic planning.

The industrial planning system inherited by Khrushchev was the direct product of Stalinist industrialisation during the 1930s. The system was both highly centralised and extremely competitive. Plans for each industry were set by the State Planning Commission (Gosplan) in Moscow. Each industry was run by a Ministry (known before World War II as Commissariats); some industries might have more than one Ministry. The engineering industry, for example, was treated as several separate industries: heavy engineering, medium-sized engineering, light engineering, automobile production, etc., each with its own Ministry. It was the Ministry's job to transmit the plan to all the sub-branches under its jurisdiction, down to each individual factory. The plan, in turn, specified every little detail about production: how much steel, coal, wood, or other materials a

Table 6.1   Industrial Production in Major Soviet Industries, 1950–1965

	1950	1955	1960	1965
Iron and steel products (million tons)				
Pig iron	19.2	33.3	46.8	66.2
Steel	27.3	45.3	65.3	91.0
Rolled steel	18.0	30.6	43.7	61.7
Steel pipe	2.0	3.5	5.8	9.0
Engineering industry				
Turbines (total capacity, million KW)	2.8	5.6	9.2	14.6
Metal-cutting machine tools (1000 units)	70.6	117.0	156.0	186.0
Forge-press equipment (1000 units)	7.7	17.1	29.9	34.6
Lorries (1000 units)	294.4	328.1	362.0	379.6
Light vehicles (1000 units)	64.6	107.8	138.8	201.2
Tractors (1000 units)	117.0	163.0	239.0	355.0
Energy and Fuel				
Electric power (million kilowatt-hrs.)	91.2	170.2	292.3	506.7
Oil (million tons)	37.9	70.8	147.9	242.9
Natural gas (billion cubic metres)	5.8	9.0	45.3	127.7
Coal (million tons)	261.1	389.9	509.6	577.7
Chemical industry				
Mineral fertilisers (million tons)	5.5	9.7	13.9	31.3
Synthetic fibres (1000 tons)	24	110	211	407
Synthetic resins and plastics (1000 tons)	67.1	160	312	803
Light industry				
Cotton cloth (million square metres)	2 745	4 227	4 838	5 499
Wool cloth (million square metres)	193	316	439	466
Linen (million square metres)	257	272	516	548
Silk cloth (million square metres)	106	415	675	801
Leather footwear (million pairs)	203	271	419	486

Source: [58: *201, 205, 206, 208, 213, 216, 220, 222, 227, 229, 245, 249*].

factory was to use; where these supplies came from; what the factory was to produce; how much it was to spend on wages; how much productivity per worker was to rise during the year; where it was to send its finished products.

This centralisation was perpetually being undermined by the system itself. Because of its bureaucratic origins, and the scarcities created or made worse by Stalin's policy of break-neck, forced industrialisation in the 1930s, every economic agency, from Ministries down to individual factories, competed against one another for resources. In the 1930s, for example, when the labour shortage was particularly acute, factories would poach each other's workers by making lavish promises of higher wages, better housing, better food, and so on – promises they often could not keep [18: 59–60]. This mentality of scarcity survived right up to the break-up of the USSR and even beyond. Ministries constantly competed against one another within the higher circles of government for more investment. Since there was only so much that could be made available for investment in a given year, each Ministry pressed its claims at the expense of others. We have already seen how Khrushchev's agricultural policies were undermined by his failure to win new investment resources for agriculture because the more powerful Ministries in charge of heavy industry (which always had priority status in the USSR) blocked attempts to take resources away from their domains.

Factories had their own ways of trying to win more resources (more machinery, new buildings, a larger labour force, etc.). An enterprise would seek permission to undertake a new investment project, say the expansion of a steel mill or foundry. It would deliberately underestimate how much it cost to carry out the project, in order to make it seem more attractive to the central planners. Once the project was approved, however, the factory would apply for the resources it actually needed – or even inflate these upwards as a protective cushion in case it encountered unforeseen delays or difficulties. It tended to get some or most of what it asked for, since the central authorities were reluctant to allow a project they had just authorised to go unfinished. If the project was, say, for a new steel mill, the planners would have planned on the new mill to be finished in so many years and then to start producing steel – and they would have begun incorporating this expected amount of new steel into future plans. If the mill were never finished, it would throw these future plans out of co-ordination for other factories which might have needed this steel. Thus the planners were likely to keep sinking more and more money and resources into this seemingly bottomless pit.

At the same time, however, factories were under other pressures from the centre, which they were always trying to circumvent. Factory managers deliberately underestimated real production capacity in an attempt to win low plan assignments from the centre. Why? Because success in the Soviet system was tied to plan fulfilment. If you were a factory manager and you did well and won constant recognition (not to mention bonuses) for plan overfulfilment, you would soon win a promotion, either to a better factory or to a good job within the Communist Party. Up until August 1991 and the failed *putsch* against Gorbachev, after which the Communist Party lost its institutional power and importance, the usual career pattern of up-and-coming Party members was to move from a low-level Party post to the managership of an industrial enterprise, from there back into a better Party job, then to managing a more prestigious enterprise, etc. If you failed to deliver the goods, however, the downward path of demotion could be just as swift and dramatic. So managers wanted low plans because they were easier to fulfil and overfulfil. Of course the centre knew this, and so the central planning agency (Gosplan) always incorporated a 'correction factor' into factory plans, to allow for how much they thought the managers were lying. But the managers knew about the 'correction factor' as well, and so made their *own* 'corrections' when revealing their capacities to the centre, trying to state them just a little lower than what the planners assumed.

There are many other devices managers used to try to make life easier for themselves, but we cannot go into them here. People have written whole books describing them [64; 63: *354–9*]. The essential point is that the plans were always losing their co-ordination from the moment they were drawn up because the information they were based on was distorted. But these distortions were usually perfectly rational from the point of view of each individual manager. He or she (and most were men) knew that materials were always in short supply and of poor quality, and that this always caused delays and breakdowns. So, if they kept plan targets low they could better adjust to crisis situations when the supplies did not show up or the machinery broke down. This was so generally the case that, ever since the First Five-Year Plan (1928–1932), Soviet industry was based on a

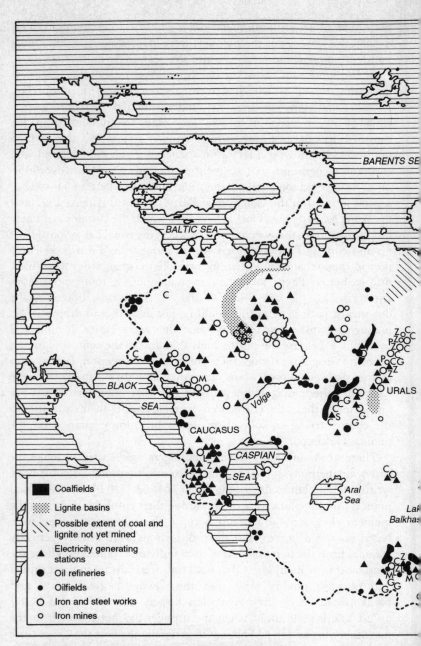

Map 3 Soviet Heavy Industry and its Raw Materials

62

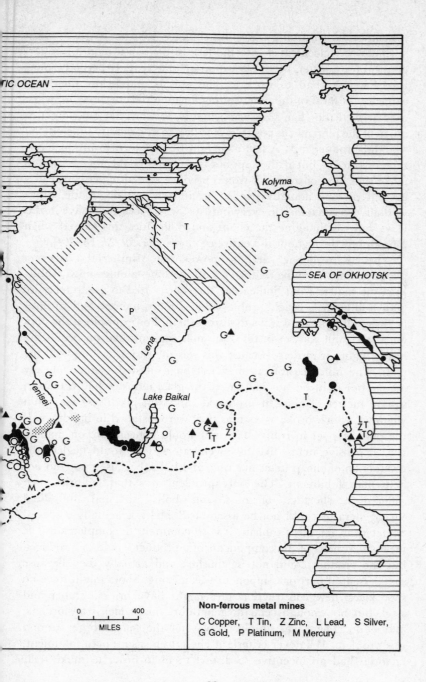

ARCTIC OCEAN

Kolyma

SEA OF OKHOTSK

Lena

Yenisei

Lake Baikal

Non-ferrous metal mines

C Copper, T Tin, Z Zinc, L Lead, S Silver,
G Gold, P Platinum, M Mercury

0   400
MILES

63

system called 'storming'. Because supplies were so irregular most output was concentrated into the last 10 days of a month, the last month of a quarter, or the last quarter of a year. Everybody knew this. Factories had to work at slow speeds and below their real capacity for most of the time waiting for materials to show up; when they arrived they had to 'storm', that is, to work flat out, to get as much of the plan met as possible. Needless to say, quality suffered. So, too, did product mix. A factory might be supposed to produce one type of tractor, but if the supplies it received could not be used to make that kind of tractor it would produce something else instead – even if no one actually needed what it eventually made. Since virtually every factory in every industry was forced to behave in this way, you can imagine the chaos and difficulties this caused when reproduced throughout the entire economy [21: *19–22*; 18: *264*].

When Khrushchev came to power the Ministerial system of planning and running industry had become almost unworkable. First, no matter what 'indicators' the centre tried to use to measure plan fulfilment – weight, ruble value, square metres, and so on – factories always found ways to distort them. For example, if the plan for a steel mill was set in tons, the mill concentrated on producing heavy ingots or girders, because this was the easiest way to fulfil the plan. The mill's customers may not have needed so many heavy ingots, but that did not matter. If the glass industry had a plan in square metres of glass, it produced (and still produces) very thin windows, which broke as soon as they were installed in buildings. If the plan was set in rubles, factories would concentrate on making very expensive items, like turbogenerators, but would neglect the production of cheap items like nuts and bolts, because these did not help plan fulfilment. The only problem was that factories then suffered a shortage of nuts and bolts, so that the final turbogenerator could not be assembled! There is actually a special Soviet term for this problem, it is so common: 'incompleteness'. It means that most of the components of a product would be produced but the product could not be finished and actually used because some essential part or component was missing. Shoes might have no shoe laces; new construction sites might have bricks, timber and steel, but not enough cement; generators might lack transformers; and so on. There was simply no way for the centre to get around this problem. Whatever criteria it chose to measure plan fulfilment, factories had an incentive to distort them in order to make their results look more favourable, even if this damaged the economy as a whole [21: *162–3*].

A second problem was that the planning system created a positive disincentive against introducing new technology. This is because any new technology, new ways of organising production, or new products always have 'teething' problems when they are first introduced. Even though in the medium or long term they might improve production, increase output or lower costs, in the short run they almost always reduce output and/or raise costs until all the kinks have been ironed out. In the Stalinist planning system this meant that during these settling-in periods a factory's plan fulfilment might go down, and managers were simply unwilling to run the risk of appearing to do their job badly [14: *322–3*]. Also, the peculiar position of workers in Soviet factories, as we shall note in the last part of this chapter, made it important for managers to retain their goodwill on the shop floor, and new technologies might have necessitated redundancies or redeployments, both of which proved difficult to impose both practically and under Soviet law. Until Gorbachev's market reforms and the adoption of a policy of creating large-scale unemployment (as a way of creating greater labour mobility and encouraging factories to cut production costs), a worker could not actually be fired except for grave violations of discipline regulations, unless management took the trouble to find him or her a new job – something most managers were not willing to do. More important, because managers needed workers' co-operation in dealing with so many other difficulties ('storming', equipment breakdowns, looking for missing tools or parts), they did not want to risk the discontent that laying people off would cause [21].

Finally, even had all managers honestly carried out their instructions, faithfully and accurately reported their true production capacities, and all workers done their jobs efficiently and conscientiously, the system still would not have worked because it was simply impossible to centralise all the millions of pieces of information needed to plan a complex industrial economy. No central planning office can collect, digest and accurately utilise that much data. It might be different if the central planners merely laid down broad guidelines for what should be done and gave enterprises the freedom to plan out themselves how they would do it, together with the resources they might need. But such ideal conditions never existed in the USSR. Instead, the Soviet Union had both extremely bureaucratic centralisation *and* a problem obtaining accurate information, because enterprise managers (and the workers underneath them) distorted instructions and passed falsified information back to the centre. The result was the dispersal of resources and investments over too many enterprises and construction projects, as managers and Ministries competed with one another for as many resources as they could claim, even if they could not utilise these resources properly. And because each part of the economy was interlinked with all the others, distortions in one area worked themselves through and caused distortions elsewhere. If a steel mill produced the wrong kind of steel, the engineering factory that used this steel produced either the wrong kind of equipment or a machine of poor quality; this poor quality machinery was then used to make other products whose quality was also bad or whose specifications did not meet those that customer factories needed. These products then passed on to the next stage in the chain, either to a consumer who received shoddy consumer goods, or to another enterprise which had to make do with inadequate or low-grade materials or equipment. And so it went on, and on, and on [21: *134–5*].

When Khrushchev came to power this system had reached such heights of absurdity that in 1955 and 1956 – before Khrushchev launched his major reform of industry – factories were actually being allocated materials from non-existent suppliers! Certain factories, when they began to wonder what had happened to their supplies sent out agents (known as 'pushers' in Russian) to try to speed up their orders. The agents in turn found that the enterprises from which they were supposed to obtain their materials had not yet been built. And this was deliberately being done by the planning authorities, who hoped that by giving the newly-constructed enterprises real production plans, the construction firms building them would work harder to have these enterprises finished on time. Of course, construction of the new factories continued to run behind schedule just as before, and so these 'enterprises' (which existed only on paper) were obviously unable to produce any of the materials or machinery that had been 'planned' for them [21: *17*].

During *perestroika* Gorbachev and his economic advisors tried to break through these long-standing problems by shifting the Soviet Union to a Western-style market economy. The theory was that if enterprises had to find their own suppliers they would demand better quality goods and prompt deliveries. If they had to find their own customers they would produce high quality products and deliver them on time. If they had to make sure they earned a profit they would be careful to keep production costs under control by modernising their equipment and laying off workers they did not actually need. This policy, too, met with little success. For instance, most factories responded to the need to earn a profit not by producing more or higher-quality goods, but simply by raising prices. The result was galloping inflation in the USSR while output actually fell and shortages grew worse, especially of much-needed consumer goods [20]. Both Khrushchev and Gorbachev had inherited a system from the leaders who had come before: Khrushchev from Stalin, Gorbachev from Khrushchev and Brezhnev. Both essentially tried to make changes in that system while still working within it, and both failed in their task.

The Sovnarkhoz Reform

Khrushchev's answer to these problems was to reorganise industry in a way that would weaken the power of the industrial Ministries. In February 1957 the government announced the reorganisation of industry into so-called Regional Economic Councils, or *sovnarkhozy* (literally, Councils of the National Economy). Under this system factories were no longer controlled by the Ministry to which they belonged, but by the Regional Council, or *sovnarkhoz*, in charge of the region in which they were located. For example, an engineering factory in Moscow, which used to come under the control of one of the appropriate engineering ministries, now was part of the Moscow *sovnarkhoz*.

The idea was that the Regional Councils could rationally co-ordinate production and distribution between all the enterprises within their region. Under the old system an engineering factory, for example, might receive steel not from a local steel mill, but from one literally at the other end of the country. By the same token, this engineering enterprise might supply machines to other factories thousands of miles away when the latter could just as easily have obtained the same machine from a local engineering works. This system arose because the Ministries in charge of each industry all had their own supply and trade organisations which did little to coordinate their efforts with those of other Ministries. Goods needlessly went back and forth across the country, running up huge transport costs with supplies often being delivered by air. Some factories in a locality would suffer shortages of an essential item while a neighbouring factory under a different Ministry had huge stockpiles of it [21: *17*].

The regime hoped that the *sovnarkhoz* reform would eliminate this waste of resources by matching up local suppliers with local customers. Engineering firms in one *sovnarkhoz* would now obtain their steel from steel mills in the same *sovnarkhoz*, instead of flying in metal from the far ends of the USSR, as was commonly the case. The regime also hoped that the *sovnarkhozy* would eliminate the wasteful competition between Ministries. *In theory* the *sovnarkhozy* would be interested in providing the most rational co-ordination between the enterprises in their region, and would not engage in the empire-building of the Ministries, with each trying to outbid the other for investment funds and resources [63: *342–4*].

Like other reforms, this one, too, was a failure. The problems it had to deal with were real enough, but, as Alec Nove has pointed out, the *sovnarkhoz* reform tried to solve them while leaving the basic system of bureaucratic planning unchanged. The parochialism of the old Ministries, whereby each Ministry tried to defend its own patch against the demands of others, was merely replaced by the parochialism and narrow-mindedness of the Regional Economic Councils. How this happened is not hard to imagine.

Each industry, for example, engineering, iron and steel, or automobiles, had factories dispersed all over the territory of the Soviet Union. Under the old system these geographically isolated factories were co-ordinated by their industrial Ministry. Now there was no co-ordination between them, since each factory came under its local Economic Council. You can imagine the problems this created with supplies and co-ordination of plans. An enterprise was no longer linked to suppliers and customers for its own products through a single Ministry. It now had to deal with enterprises subordinated to dozens of different *sovnarkhozy*, thus multiplying the amount of bureaucratic red tape it had to go through when dealing with other enterprises in its own branch of production. By the same token, a *sovnarkhoz* might meddle in production plans and disrupt the production of supplies for factories in other *sovnarkhozy* in order to give preference to factories in its own locality. For example, if an engineering factory making a certain type of machine had previously received motors from a supplier located in another region, it now had to enter into complex negotiations with the *sovnarkhoz* in which this supplier now found itself. This *sovnarkhoz*, in its turn, might easily decide that it wanted these motors for a factory in its own territory, and so would block their delivery to the first engineering firm [52: *106*; 63: *359*].

The result was bureaucratic anarchy. Many factories which used to receive parts or supplies from factories in other regions now had to try to make these things themselves. But because they were not set up for this and did not have the specialised equipment or supplies that were needed, they could produce them only very inefficiently and expensively. This diverted workers, materials and equipment away from producing the things these factories were supposed to produce, so the factory's production and the economy as a whole suffered [21: *26–8*].

These drawbacks of the *sovnarkhoz* reform soon became obvious. But instead of withdrawing the reform, the government tried to deal with it in piecemeal fashion by creating new, central bureaucratic bodies that existed parallel to the *sovnarkhozy*. Soon an entire new bureaucratic network of planning agencies grew up, all located in Moscow and designed to overcome the problems created by the localism of the *sovnarkhozy*: State Committees, Central Councils, a Supreme Economic Council, and a reorganisation of the State Planning Commission (Gosplan). The *sovnarkhozy* themselves were consolidated into larger *sovnarkhozy*. All this new bureaucracy merely made matters worse. The *sovnarkhozy* still existed, but the new Moscow-based agencies, especially the State Committees, started to assume the functions of the old Ministries. So, instead of one cumbersome bureaucracy there were now several. No one knew where authority really lay. In the words of the Medvedevs [52: *107*]:

As a result, by 1963 the bureaucratic apparatus for 'managing' industry not only had not been reduced, as had been intended by the concept of 'decentralisation', but had almost tripled. Instead of American-style competition, the evils of duplication, parallelism, and dissipation of responsibility were the result. The rate of modernisation declined, the list of shortages grew longer, while warehouses were bulging with unsold, outmoded goods scorned by the consumer. Industrial management had been transformed into a labyrinth of interrelationships with multiple administrations and departments. One often had to wait months to get an answer to an urgent question about everyday procedure. Thus the 'new system for managing industry' had brought the nation to an impasse, and there was no obvious way out.

It is important to keep in mind, however, that the *sovnarkhoz* reform failed not simply because it was poorly thought out. To an even greater extent it was a casualty of the bureaucratic planning system itself. If before, under the old ministerial system, the individual Ministries jockeyed for position at the expense of each other, under the reform this same logic was simply transferred to the new *sovnarkhozy*. Each carried out its work with one main aim: how to make itself look successful in terms of plan fulfilment *for its own enterprises*, even if this made life extremely difficult for other sectors of the economy. Factory managers were still faced with serious problems of acquiring supplies and having superiors interfere with their production plans. So bad did the situation become that managers often by-passed official supply channels and engaged in direct barter with one another, swapping, for example, surplus steel for machinery or building materials [21: *21*]. Thus the *sovnarkhoz* reform brought real co-ordination of a complex industrial economy no nearer. Upon Khrushchev's downfall in October 1964 the *sovnarkhoz* reform was one of the first things the new leadership changed. Yet none of the further 'reforms' they put in its place helped solve the main problems facing the Soviet economy.

Labour Policy

Since the beginnings of Stalinist industrialisation, one of the main difficulties facing the Soviet economy has been the poor on-the-job performance of industrial workers. To some extent this has been conditioned by the general disruptions that factories have to confront on a day-to-day basis, which make it difficult rationally to organise and co-ordinate production schedules and which cause countless interruptions to the work routine as workers have to leave off what they are doing to hunt down missing parts or tools, wait for job assignments, or decipher unclear or incorrect plans and drawings. However, the workers themselves have played a large part in causing, or at least perpetuating such disruptions. Why? The answer lies largely in the fact that as Stalin and his supporters consolidated their power in the late 1920s and early 1930s and the country came under increasingly authoritarian rule, ordinary people in both towns and countryside were excluded from any say in how society was to be run. On the contrary, they were subjected to terrible material hardship and brutal repression if they protested. At work it became more and more difficult to protest against government policies, especially the intensification of work speeds and wage cuts that were regularly imposed in the 1930s. However, workers discovered that they had one countervailing power with which to defend themselves. Because the economy was always desperately short of labour, managers found that they had to reach some form of accommodation with their workers in order to keep them from quitting or to persuade them to help ease the many difficulties that routinely threatened a factory's production programme. The main concessions that managers made were over work speeds, quality, and to some extent wages. Workers were allowed, within limits of course, to slow down the pace of work and to ignore quality demands. When speed up and wage cuts became too great, as during the Stakhanov movement in the mid-1930s, managers also helped ease the burdens by lowering output quotas (known as 'norms' in Russian) and subsidising wages through semi-legal or even illegal bonuses [18].

Khrushchev, as we have noted, was well aware that if the economic situation was going to improve he would have to win the co-operation of the industrial workforce, partly through persuasion and improvements in workers' morale, and partly by putting pressure on workers to work harder. The latter he tried to do by recasting the wages and incentives system. As with other areas of social and economic policy, the problem proved more intractable than the leadership imagined. What is more, in trying to solve one set of problems Khrushchev's labour policies created others that were equally as damaging to the drive to achieve a more efficient economy.

Soon after the Secret Speech Khrushchev introduced a number of morale-boosting measures designed to reduce workers' feelings of alienation on the shop floor and in society at large. In April 1956 the government repealed the draconian Stalinist labour laws of June 1940, which had made it a criminal offence to change jobs or commit absenteeism. These laws had already been partially liberalised in 1951 and 1952; their continued ineffectiveness was demonstrated by the increasing unwillingness of lower courts and factory managers to enforce them. Thus their repeal in 1956 was both politically consistent with the new liberalisation and a tacit admission that the laws were an obstacle to economic progress [23; 21: *36–41*]. Along with the changes in labour law, 1957–1958 saw a reform of the trade unions. Since the 1920s Soviet trade unions had ceased to defend the collective interests of their members, and had acted more or less as a 'transmission belt', helping to implement economic policy on the shop floor. Until the mid-1930s, however, they had been allowed to exercise some independence at local level when it came to defending individual workers from dismissal. The Khrushchev trade union reform restored to the unions their right to veto managerial orders to fire workers and orders to raise output quotas. Although the number of workers protesting managerial abuses in these areas was relatively small, those who did object now stood a good chance of succeeding. Thus the unions now became more willing to defend individual workers over specific grievances, even if they still did not represent the *collective* interests of their members against factory management or the government [41: *66–70*; 21: *39, 43*].

The other side of this policy was a reform of the wages system. By the time Khrushchev came to power the various abuses of wages regulations used by managers to protect workers' earnings had achieved a near epic scale. It was generally accepted that no one could live off of their officially-prescribed wages, and so fiddles in the form of low output quotas and various bonuses for fictitious work were common. The wage reform of 1956–1962 tried to change this. Firstly, it tried to make the system more 'fair' by raising the minimum wage and narrowing differentials between unskilled and skilled workers. At the same time the new rules made it harder to pay workers bonuses. Those bonuses that were to be paid would come not from overfulfilling quotas, but for general factory plan fulfilment or for improving the quality of products and helping to cut production costs. The reform did help reduce general overspending of industry's total wages fund, but it did little to improve workers' incentives to work better. For one thing, many workers, especially skilled manual workers, lost out in the reform, and managers had to find new loopholes to protect their earnings for fear they might quit. Secondly, the money made available to pay the new quality bonuses was too small, and so workers found little incentive to make improvements in this area [36; 19].

Another problem with the reform was its failure to reduce wage inequalities. Although the differentials between skilled and unskilled within each industry were somewhat narrowed, inequalities between industries remained large. The best-paid worker in the food industry, for example, earned but one-third of the best-paid worker in coal mining or oil extraction. Because of such huge gaps between one industry and another, many enterprises found it hard to hold on to their workers, who would quit to seek better pay at other factories in the same locality [21: *104–7*; 82: *141–5*].

The one branch of industry where the wage reform really did tighten up on earnings was engineering, and here its strict implementation caused such a crisis that the cure became worse than the disease. Machine tool operators (turners, drill operators, press operators, and similar trades) found that because their jobs were relatively highly mechanised it was easier for management to calculate and impose fairly rigid output quotas. Similarly, for reasons that are not clear, the reform reclassified most of them into the lowest wage and skill grades, meaning that they earned less than workers in other industries for doing jobs at comparable levels of skill and intensity. The result was a mass exodus of workers from these jobs – the most important trade in engineering. Factories found it nearly impossible to recruit enough machine tool operators to run all of their equipment. When they did recruit new workers, many quit at the first opportunity as soon as they saw how little they were earning relative to the amount of effort they now had to put in. Machinists preferred skilled manual jobs, such as fitters who assembled or repaired equipment, because here they earned more money and had greater control over how fast they worked. But machinists were also willing to move into unskilled jobs, even at lower pay, if the pace of work was easier. It also became difficult to persuade school-leavers to take up apprenticeships as machine tool operators, since they now viewed it as a trade with low pay and low prestige. So serious did the situation in engineering become that almost as soon as Khrushchev was removed from office his successors repealed the wage reform and allowed wages in engineering to rise substantially. Only then was the shortage of machinists finally solved [3: *71—6*; 21: *75–89*].

Khrushchev's labour policies encountered difficulties in other areas, as well. One of the centre-pieces of Khrushchev's industrial policy was the proposed industrial development of Siberia and the Far Eastern regions of the USSR. These areas were rich in raw materials, and their shipment westward into the industrial heartlands of Russia, Ukraine, and Belorussiya was costly and inefficient. It made more sense to bring industry to the sources of the raw materials. At the same time such a policy, it was hoped, would achieve a more even distribution of the urban population across the USSR's territory and relieve the pressures on housing and services in the older urban centres of Moscow and Leningrad. To this end the 1950s saw a major campaign to recruit young people to come work in Siberia to help put up new factories and then to settle there as part of the permanent population. In a way the development of Siberia was the industrial equivalent to the Virgin Lands campaign, and the regime placed great faith in its success as part of its overall strategy for improving the country's industrial performance.

Like so many other policies, however, this one, too, foundered on its poor preparation. It was fairly easy to attract people, especially young workers and students, to give a few years to the Siberian development campaign, but if they were to be persuaded to stay they would need housing, roads, good access to food supplies, and cultural amenities such as cinemas, libraries and theatres. But the development plans almost totally ignored this side of things. Workers had to put up with harsh conditions in primitive barracks. Some building sites did not even have access to a cafeteria or canteen: their workers had to travel two hours in the morning to another settlement just to have breakfast. Combined with Siberia's harsh climate, it became difficult to persuade people to stay. Many left even before their initial contracts ran out. Some building projects lost most of their recruits within a year of their arrival. Overall this period saw a net population loss in Siberia, meaning that more people left to go back to the industrialised parts of the USSR than could be recruited to take their place. And because conditions were so difficult, it became almost impossible to persuade local women to enter industry to help make up the shortage. They had to stay at home and tend the private plot to help supplement food supplies or to look after young children because child-care facilities were so inadequate [21: *66–70*; 37; 66: *100*].

The regime's failure to recruit and retain a stable working population in Siberia considerably set back its plans for developing this region. To be fair, this problem was not unique to the Khrushchev period: Siberia is still underdeveloped relative to its potential. But the failure of the recruitment campaign is illustrative of the way in which the Khrushchev regime attempted to solve most major problems.

One section of the industrial workforce found life especially difficult in these years, namely women [21: *177–208*]. Compared to the West, women made up a large proportion of industrial workers – nearly half – but this did not mean that they necessarily enjoyed greater equality of opportunity. As in the West, women tended to be confined to certain 'feminised' industries like textiles, the garment industry, knitwear, and food, where wages were low and the intensity of labour very high [21: *180, 193–6*; 82: *141–5*]. Where women worked alongside men in industries where they are generally under-represented in capitalist countries, for example, in engineering or chemicals, here, too, they were restricted to the lowest-paying, most monotonous jobs [77: *57, 84*]. In all industries women made up the overwhelming bulk of workers doing unmechanised, heavy manual labour [5: *106*]. These jobs were strenuous and usually (but not always) low-paid, and subjected women to a number of health hazards [13; 32]. Moreover, as manual jobs became mechanised women tended to be pushed out of them and these jobs were given to men [5: *115*; 77: *63–4*]. At the other extreme, women were an almost insignificant share of skilled manual occupations, such as setters of machine tools or repair and maintenance mechanics [5: *106, 115*; 77: *57–8, 63–4, 84*; 38: *50–1*; 47: *210–11*]. In almost all cases women earned only about two-thirds of what men earned, even where they had more schooling and experience [65: *37, 40*; 77: *78*].

Women workers suffered heavily from their so-called 'double burden'. The overwhelming majority of Soviet women work, often in jobs (such as textiles) where the speed and stress levels are far higher than those that male workers have to put up with. They also have to do virtually all of the housework (in this regard little has changed since Khrushchev's time). Under Soviet conditions this meant that a married women with one or two children was spending almost as much time looking after the home as she was at the factory: queuing to buy food, cooking, washing up, cleaning the flat, looking after the children, even repairing the furniture. In Moscow, for example, the average married woman put in some 35 hours a week on domestic labour and seeing to her own personal needs, versus just 14 hours for men. Outside of Moscow the domestic burden – and the discrepancy between the sexes – was even greater [78: *52*; 38: Appendix, Table 4]. It is not surprising, then, that compared to their husbands, Soviet women had little opportunity to upgrade their skills and earn promotion at work. Their situation was made more difficult by the poor state of Soviet services and consumer goods. In Khrushchev's time few families had even a refrigerator, much less a washing machine (those washing machines that existed were not automatic, clothes had to be loaded, rinsed, and mangled by hand) [5: *205*; 13: *54*]. There were not enough child-care places relative to the large demand for them, so many families had to work separate shifts and saw each other only on weekends [67: *98*; 83: *154*; 21: *201*]. And the general shortages of food meant that shopping was extremely time-consuming, as women had to stand in long queues for even the most basic items. Time wasted queuing was made even longer by the failure to pre-package goods. Such basic items as eggs, pasta, and even milk were usually sold unpackaged, so that shoppers had to wait for them to be measured out, weighed and priced, which dragged out the agonies of shopping even further [77: *165–6*].

Women workers were not an example of a policy that 'failed'. The fact was that in this area of economic and social life the Khrushchev regime had no policy. This was its problem. On the one hand, it drew considerable benefits from the fact that millions of women worked in highly-intensive, low-paid industries, which in effect helped subsidise the wastage and inefficiencies incurred elsewhere. On the other hand, its neglect of women's living and working conditions meant that nearly half its workforce were functioning at below their potential productive capacity because of excessive strain and fatigue both at home and in the factory. Moreover, the Khrushchev regime's main solution for solving the labour shortage of these years was a campaign to draw more women into production. Its success here was limited precisely because for many women it was simply not worth leaving the home to take up a job in unpleasant conditions with low pay, especially when there was a shortage of child care places [21: *62–5*]. In this regard the regime's disregard for the well-being of women workers proved another obstacle to its policies of industrial development.

7 The Reorganisation of the Communist Party

During the years of Stalin's rule real power in the Soviet Union resided not in the government, but in the upper echelons of the Communist Party. In fact, until World War II, Stalin never held any formal government office. His power came from his post as Party General Secretary. Policy was discussed and made in the Politburo and, to a lesser extent, in the Central Committee. The party bureaucracy controlled all major appointments to Party and government posts (the so-called *nomenklatura*). Equally as important, the Party was responsible for overseeing the execution of policy through its local branches and cells. The Party carried out a similar role in the Brezhnev years [42: *176*]. Yet, as surprising as it may seem, during the last years of Stalin's life the Party had relatively little influence. Power resided in Stalin's personal Secretariat, which oversaw all the different functions of government and management of the economy. It was Khrushchev who placed the Party back in the centre of the political stage. Here he had two motivations. First, Khrushchev used the Party as his base of political power. Secondly, he was well aware of the conservatism and inertia of the existing governmental and ministerial bureaucracies, and thought that through the Party he could revitalise popular morale and initiative, while still keeping such initiative under tight control [42: *178*].

As already noted, Khrushchev's rise to power in many ways mirrored that of Stalin. Khrushchev used his position as the First Secretary of the Party's Central Committee to promote or appoint to positions of power and responsibility – and hence also of privilege – people who would then support him in his struggles against his opponents. Some of these were old allies from his days as Communist Party boss in Moscow or Ukraine; others were people whom his rivals had somehow offended; still others were young Communist officials who, through Khrushchev, were able to enter the ranks of the ruling elite. Naturally, this process took time, but by 1957 and his battle against the 'Anti-Party Group', Khrushchev's supporters were a majority of the Central Committee and its Presidium [69: 56–7]. Of course this network of appointments would have been meaningless if the jobs these people received had not carried any authority. Thus the other side of Khrushchev's strategy was to revitalise the Communist Party and make it once more the supreme power in the land. Khrushchev did this first, by enhancing the importance of the Central Committee, so that it became the country's main policy-making organ, and second, by decentralising economic authority down to republican and regional level, with power now in the hands of local Party bodies, rather than local councils (soviets) [69: 57–8].

We have already seen how Khrushchev used the Party in this way when he placed collective farms under the control of the Machine-Tractor Stations. Even after the MTS were abolished and responsibility for agricultural management was given back to local council executive committees, the Party still exercised control, since these executive committees were headed up by local Party officials. What is more, the 1950s saw a large increase in Communist Party membership among *kolkhoz* and *sovkhoz* Party organisations, so that even with the administrative changes, the Party, in marked contrast to the Stalin period, was firmly entrenched in local rural affairs [68: 333]. Later on, agriculture was put under the control of so-called Territorial Production Associations, which, too, were run by local Party bodies [55: 131; 76: 110–11]. The situation was similar with the *sovnarkhoz* reform, which greatly enhanced the power of local party sections [69: 57–8].

If this system of patronage had been crucial to Khrushchev's rise to power, once he had consolidated that power he resorted to frequent shake-ups, removing large numbers of his own appointees at both national and local level. At first sight this appears illogical. Why antagonise the people who have kept you in power? To some extent, Khrushchev removed people as scapegoats for policy failures. At the same time, he very likely wanted to make sure that the local officials on whom he depended did not themselves become too powerful [44: 23; 1: 145–7].

This perhaps explains why Khrushchev adopted two major reforms of the Communist Party which greatly alienated his previous supporters and helped lead to his downfall.

The first of these we have already mentioned: at the Twenty-

Second Party Congress in 1961 Khrushchev imposed so-called Rule 25, which limited the number of years a Party official could stay in office. This rule called for one-third of Party officials to be replaced at each election, from low-level district Party committees on through the regional (*oblast'*) committees, right up to the Central Committee itself (but not, significantly, including the Communist Party's First Secretary, Khrushchev's job).

This change provoked intense resentment for obvious reasons, since those officials who might lose their jobs would also lose the privileges that went with them. In many ways it is difficult the understand why Khrushchev pushed through this rule. A number of people have argued that he did it not in the interests of making the system more 'democratic' (in theory if officials had only a short period in office they would behave less bureaucratically and dictatorially), but simply to be able to control local Party officials more closely [52: *151–2*; 44: *21, 23*]. Yet Khrushchev was clearly running a great political risk here, which his years as absolute ruler had surely led him to underestimate. He had come to power precisely by using his position as Party First Secretary to appoint a new generation of regional Party officials who owed their loyalty to him. It should have been obvious that if he threatened the interests and privileges of these people they would turn against him, as they eventually did.

A much more sweeping change occurred in November 1962, when Khrushchev reorganised the Communist Party into two sections: one in charge of industry and one in charge of agriculture [52: *153–8*; 50: *204–6*; 55: *130–2*]. To some extent this reform was an extension of the reorganisation of industry into *sovnarkhozy* and the removal of the national and Republican agricultural ministries to rural localities.

Under this reform every regional Party committee (the *obkom* – short for *oblast'* committee in Russian) and corresponding regional executive committee (in charge of the day-to-day work of the regional committee) was split in two, one responsible for industrial matters, the other for agriculture. The main casualty of this change was agriculture. The agriculture committees had few financial and organisational resources. For example, it had always been common for industrial workers to help out with essential agricultural jobs, mainly at harvest time, when the farms found themselves short-handed. This mobilisation was organised by each local Communist Party. Now, however, the regional, or *oblast'* committees in charge of industry had no interest in assisting agriculture, since this took workers away from their jobs in industry, which was now all that these industrial committees cared about. The result was a severe shortage of workers for such vital agricultural jobs as hay mowing, collecting the harvest, digging potatoes, picking vegetables, and the like. Many crops simply rotted in the fields. The response of the regional agricultural committees was to *increase* pressure on the *kolkhozniki*, in particular by making it more difficult for them to work on their household plots and private livestock, as a way of making them put more time into jobs on the *kolkhoz*. The result, as we have seen when discussing agriculture, was terribly ineffective [52: *154*].

In addition, the split of regional committees into industrial and agricultural committees led to confusion over who was to provide agriculture with what supplies. There were no clear lines of demarcation. Agricultural regional committees were made respon- sible for *factories* serving farms or processing agricultural produce. Yet the industrial regional committees were put in charge of a number of services vital to agriculture, but over which the agricultural regional committees now had no control: training schools for teachers in both urban and *rural* schools; communal garages which also serviced grain elevators; and the factories manufacturing packing materials, many of which were vital to farm work. Because of this confusion of responsibilities, the organisation of transport for harvests – which usually meant borrowing equipment from factories – became equally chaotic [50: *204*].

In line with this reorganisation the central Party structures were split, so that the Party Central Committee now had a Bureau for Agriculture and a Bureau for Industry. These existed parallel to each other, although nominally both were responsible to Khrushchev in his capacity as Party First Secretary.

At the same time Khrushchev changed the district-level Party structure in charge of agriculture (see the Party structure details on p. vii: the district – or *raion* in Russian – is the lowest territorial Party unit, and is subordinate to the region, or *oblast'*). Districts were consolidated, basically doubling the number of inhabitants and the number of collective farms in each. But this led to further problems: the new district structures now had to administer vastly larger areas, with many of the new district centres now situated far from some of the *kolkhozy* they had to manage. But because the road network was so bad and communications in general were so poor, this led to a breakdown of communications not just for ordinary residents of

80

kolkhozy or *sovkhozy* who might need to travel to a district centre on some form of business, but also for *kolkhoz* and *sovkhoz* administrators. Here the backwardness of the economy undermined an administrative reorganisation that might under other circumstances have been sensible [52: *155*]. As with the *sovnarkhoz* reform of industry, this reorganisation of the Party caused clear lines of authority to be undermined. Each *oblast'* now had two Party Secretaries: one in charge of agriculture and the other in charge of industry. Who had the final say? It was not clear. What is more, each of them was now responsible to a different section of the Party Central Committee in Moscow: the Bureau for Agriculture or the Bureau for Industry.

This in turn led to rivalries between these regional Party Secretaries over elections to the Central Committees and Supreme Soviets of the USSR or its individual Republics. Up until its transformation into a genuine law-making parliament in 1989, the Supreme Soviet had little real power in the Soviet system, but election to it was a sign of prestige. Now instead of one or two people vying for this honour, the chairpersons of the two *oblast'* committees (industry and agriculture) and the two *oblast'* executive committees were all competing against one another [52: *156–7*].

The reasons behind this reorganisation have been subject to differing interpretations. Some have argued that it was both a logical consequence of the move back towards a recentralisation of top-level control over the economy and an attempt by Khrushchev to expand his patronage base [4: *107–8, 126*; 30: *39*]. Others claim that, like with the changes in the Party rules, Khrushchev was trying to weaken the stratum of regional party officials lest they become too powerful [1: *145–7*]. There is truth in both views. Almost as soon as Khrushchev was ousted the new leadership reunited the Party structure, on the grounds of its alleged inefficiency. In reality, however, there had been almost no opposition to Khrushchev's scheme from within the Presidium, partly because it actually enhanced the power and authority of many at the top [80: *249–60*]. No, the real opposition to the reform came from the local officials themselves, since it was their position which had been undermined. Basically, the *oblast'* committee Secretaries ceased to be king in their regions, and they did not like it. 'The kings,' note the Medvedevs, 'wanted the return of their kingdoms, even if it meant sacrificing the emperor [52: *158*].'

8 Conclusion

We can summarise the basic dilemma of Khrushchev's reforms in a series of simple propositions.

Khrushchev, like Gorbachev in the post-Brezhnev era, recognised that the system had to be made more efficient. This meant:

1. . He had to do away with the worst excesses of the Stalinist system: the arbitrary secret police; the competitive in-fighting between vested interests inside the Communist Party; the empire-building and bureaucratic conservatism of the Ministries.

2. He had to motivate the population by making them feel they no longer had to live in fear, that living standards would rise, and that the system would become more open. He wanted workers and peasants to feel they now had a stake in the system.

3. He had to do all this *without fundamentally changing the system*. Thus, there would still be a Communist Party, which would continue to determine how the country was run. There would still be a large bureaucracy, but it would be run more efficiently and humanely and with more committed people. There would still be managers of factories and collective farms, who would continue to enjoy substantial privileges.

In other words, the system would remain, and it would still be based on the principle that those in charge, be they Communist Party officials, government administrators, or economic managers, would exist as a privileged group relative to the rest of the population. But the system would – or so Khrushchev and other reformers hoped – be fairer and more responsive to the complaints and wishes of ordinary people. But these ordinary people would still be without any political power.

If our interpretation here is correct, Khrushchev's problem was this: he wanted to reform the bureaucracy in order to make the bureaucracy's rule over the rest of society more secure. But this meant threatening the privileges and positions of many individual bureaucrats. If you are a Party or local government official it does you no good to learn that you are being fired because you are inefficient or corrupt, or because your part of the bureaucracy is no longer needed – all with the explanation that this is for the long-term good of the bureaucracy as a whole. You are only interested in your own individual job and privileges. And so many of those who were to be the victims of Khrushchev's reforms did everything in their power to block them. This proved his ultimate undoing.

On 13 October 1964 the Presidium removed Khrushchev from power – a decision that was probably popular with most Soviet citizens [50: *235–45*]. The promises of de-Stalinisation had been largely still-born. Living standards had not continued to improve after the initial progress of the mid-1950s. Khrushchev's own impetuous methods had clearly led to economic difficulties in both industry and agriculture. It is important to note, however, that Khrushchev's successors had little positive to put in his place. The Brezhnev period amounted to nearly two decades of stagnation, corruption and increasing repression.

In the end Khrushchev's failure was not his penchant for 'hare-brained schemes', the naive trust he placed in irresponsible advisors and officials, or even his blustery, authoritarian methods of rule. His failure was that he proved unable fundamentally to alter the inner workings of the Soviet bureaucratic system. To a large degree this system defeated even the best-intentioned and best-thought-out of his reforms because they challenged the privileges of the very people who were supposed to implement them. At a deeper level Khrushchev was willing to challenge some *features* of the system, but not the system itself. Indeed, he was a product of that system and owed his own position to it. As a French political philosopher asked at the time, who was going to de-Stalinise the de-Stalinisers?

The experience of Khrushchev leads us to an even more basic question. Could the Stalinist system be reformed and still remain intact? Certainly Gorbachev believed that it was possible, but that the reforms would have to be bolder and more consistently applied. His own failure suggests that perhaps Khrushchev's rivals – Kaganovich, Molotov and Malenkov – had been justified when, in 1956, they feared that de-Stalinisation would set in motion a chain of events that would eventually sweep them all from power. The bureaucratic system was strong enough to contain that first wave of reform, but *perestroika* crossed the threshold beyond which the ruling elite could no longer control the speed and direction of the changes it had unleashed. Were the conservatives right? This would truly be one of the great ironies of history. But what was the alternative? If left untouched the Soviet system was doomed to limp along in a state of near-perpetual crisis. Yet any meaningful reform would sweep away the system, and its reformers along with it.

Bibliography

[1] Jeremy R. Azrael, *Managerial Power and Soviet Politics* (Cambridge, Mass., 1966).

[2] Vadim Belotserkovsky, 'Workers' Struggles in the USSR in the Early Sixties', *Critique*, no. 10/11 (1979), pp. 37–50.

[3] L. S. Blyakhman, A. G. Zdravomyslov, and O. I. Shkaratan, *Dvizhenie rabochei sily na promyshlennykh predpriyatiyakh* (Moscow, 1965).

[4] George W. Breslauer, *Khrushchev and Brezhnev as Leaders: Building Authority in Soviet Politics* (London, 1982).

[5] S. V. Brova, *Sotsial'nye problemy zhenskogo truda v promyshlennosti. Po materialam sotsiologicheskikh issledovanii na predpriyatiyakh Sverdlovskoi i Chelyabinskoi oblastei.* Candidate Dissertation, Ural'skii Gosudarstvennyi Universitet im. A. M. Gor'kogo (Sverdlovsk, 1968).

[6] Wlodzimierz Brus, *Socialist Ownership and Political Systems* (London, 1975).

[7] Fedor Burlatskii, 'Khrushchev: Shtrikhi k politicheskomy portrety', *Literaturnaya gazeta*, 24 February 1988.

[8] Robert Conquest, *Power and Policy in the USSR: The Study of Soviet Dynastics* (London, 1962).

[9] Robert Conquest, *The Harvest of Sorrow: Soviet Collectivization and the Terror-Famine* (New York, 1986).

[10] Edward Crankshaw, *Khrushchev's Russia* (Harmondsworth, 1959).

[11] Edward Crankshaw, *Khrushchev* (London, 1966).

[12] Robert V. Daniels, 'The Critical Intelligentsia and the Failure of Reform', in Francesca Gori, ed., *Il XX Congresso del Pcus* (Milan, 1988), pp. 131–49.

[13] E. Z. Danilova, *Sotsial'nye problemy truda zhenshchiny-rabotnitsy* (Moscow, 1968).

[14] R. W. Davies, 'The Reappraisal of Industry', *Soviet Studies*, January 1956, pp. 308–31.

[15] Isaac Deutscher, 'The Beria Affair', in *Heretics and Renegades and Other Essays* (London, 1955), pp. 173–90.

[16] Isaac Deutscher, 'Khrushchev on Stalin', in *Ironies of History* (Oxford, 1966), pp. 3–17.

[17] Isaac Deutscher, *Marxism, Wars and Revolutions: Essays from Four Decades* (London, 1984).

[18] Donald Filtzer, *Soviet Workers and Stalinist Industrialization: The Formation of Modern Soviet Production Relations, 1928–1941* (London, 1986).

[19] Donald Filtzer, 'The Soviet Wage Reform of 1956–1962', *Soviet Studies*, vol. xli, no. 1, 1989, pp. 88–110.

85

[20]   Donald Filtzer, 'The Contradictions of the Marketless Market: Self-Financing in the Soviet Industrial Enterprise, 1986–1990', *Soviet Studies*, vol. 43, no. 6, 1991, pp. 989–1009.

[21]   Donald Filtzer, *Soviet Workers and De-Stalinization: The Consolidation of the Modern System of Soviet Production Relations, 1953–1964* (Cambridge, 1992).

[22]   Mark Frankland, *Khrushchev* (New York, 1969).

[23]   Jerzy Gliksman, 'Recent Trends in Soviet Labor Legislation', *Problems of Communism*, July–August 1956, pp. 20–28.

[24]   Francesca Gori, ed., *Il XX Congresso del Pcus* (Milan, 1988)

[25]   W. G. Hahn, *The Politics of Soviet Agriculture* (Baltimore, 1972).

[26]   Gundula Helmert, 'The Reflection of Working Life in the Teaching Programmes of Soviet Non-Specialist Schools, 1928–1940', unpublished conference paper, Centre for Russian and East European Studies, University of Birmingham, June 1981.

[27]   Gundula Helmert, *Schuler unter Stalin 1928–1940. Über den Zusammenhang von Massenbildung und Herrschaftsinteressen*, Ph.D. thesis, Gesamthochschule Kassel, 1982.

[28]   M. Holubenko, 'The Soviet Working Class: Discontent and Opposition', *Critique*, no. 4 (1975), pp. 5–25.

[29]   Geoffrey Hosking, *A History of the Soviet Union* (London, 1985).

[30]   Willian Hyland and Richard Wallace Shryock, *The Fall of Khrushchev* (London, 1970).

[31]   Boris Kagarlitsky, *Farewell Perestroika: A Soviet Chronicle* (London, 1990).

[32]   N. P. Kalinina, *Usloviya truda i osnovnye napravleniya ikh uluchsheniya na predpriyatiyakh tekstil'noi promyshlennosti* (Moscow, 1969).

[33]   J. F. Karcz, *The Economics of Communist Agriculture* (Bloomington, 1979).

[34]   N. S. Khrushchev, *Khrushchev Remembers*, with an Introduction, Commentary and Notes by Edward Crankshaw (London, 1971).

[35]   Sergei Khrushchev, *Khrushchev on Khrushchev: An Inside Account of the Man and His Era, by His Son* (Boston, 1992).

[36]   Leonard Joel Kirsch, *Soviet Wages: Changes in Structure and Administration* (Cambridge, Mass., 1972).

[37]   I. I. Komogortsev, *Promyshlennost' i rabochii klass Sibiri v period stroitel'stva kommunizma (1959–1965 gg)* (Novosibirsk, 1971).

[38]   I. I. Korobitsyna, *Zhenskii trud v sisteme obshchestvennogo truda pri sotsializme*. Candidate dissertation, Sverdlovskii gosudarstvennyi yuridicheskii institut, 1966.

[39]   Bill Lomax, *Hungary 1956* (London, 1976).

[40]   Alastair McAuley, 'Social Policy', in Martin McCauley, ed., *Khrushchev and Khrushchevism* (London, 1987), pp. 138–55.

[41]   Mary McAuley, *Labour Disputes in Soviet Russia, 1957–1965* (Oxford, 1969).

[42]   Mary McAuley, *Politics and the Soviet Union* (Harmandsworth, 1978).

[43]   Martin McCauley, *Khrushchev and the Development of Soviet Agriculture: The Virgin Land Programme, 1953–1964* (London, 1976).

[44] Martin McCauley, 'Khrushchev as Leader', in Martin McCauley, ed., *Khrushchev and Khrushchevism* (London, 1987), pp. 9–29.

[45] Martin McCauley, *Nikita Sergeevich Khrushchev* (London, 1991).

[46] Martin McCauley, ed., *Khrushchev and Khrushchevism* (London, 1987).

[47] N. P. Maloletova, *Rabochie legkoi promyshlennosti SSSR v 1945–1965 g.g. (chislennost' i sostav)*. Candidate dissertation (Moscow, 1970).

[48] Mervyn Matthews, *Class and Society in Soviet Russia* (London, 1972).

[49] Roy A. Medvedev, *All Stalin's Men* (Oxford, 1983).

[50] Roy A. Medvedev, *Khrushchev* (Oxford, 1983).

[51] Roy A. Medvedev, *Let History Judge* (Oxford, 1989).

[52] Roy A. Medvedev and Zhores A. Medvedev, *Khrushchev: The Years in Power* (Oxford, 1977).

[53] Zhores A. Medvedev, *The Rise and Fall of T. D. Lysenko* (New York, 1969).

[54] Zhores. A. Medvedev, *Soviet Agriculture* (New York, 1987).

[55] Robert F. Miller, 'Khrushchev and the Soviet Economy: Management by Re-organization', in R. F. Miller and F. Féhér, eds, *Khrushchev and the Communist World* (London, 1984), pp. 108–38.

[56] R. F. Miller and F. Féhér, eds, *Khrushchev and the Communist World* (London, 1984).

[57] *Narodnoe khozyaistvo SSSR v 1965 g. (Moscow, 1966).*

[58] *Narodnoe khozyaistvo SSSR za 60 let* (Moscow, 1977).

[59] Aleksandr M. Nekrich, 'The Socio-Political Effects of Khrushchev: His Impact on Soviet Intellectual Life', in R. F. Miller and F. Féhér, eds, *Khrushchev and the Communist World* (London, 1984), pp. 82–107.

[60] *Nikita Sergeevich Khrushchev: Materialy k biografii* (Moscow, 1989).

[61] Joseph L. Nogee and Robert H. Donaldson, *Soviet Foreign Policy Since World War II* (Oxford, 1984).

[62] Alec Nove, 'Wages in the Soviet Union: A Comment on Recently Published Statistics', *British Journal of Industrial Relations*, July 1966, pp. 212–21.

[63] Alec Nove, *An Economic History of the USSR* (Harmondsworth, 1969).

[64] Alec Nove, *The Soviet Economic System* (London, 1977).

[65] E. P. Ovchinnikova, and S. V. Brova, 'O likvidatsii ostatkov sotsial'nogo neravenstva rabochikh u rabotnits na promyshlennykh predpriyatiyakh', in *Protsessy izmeneniya sotsial'noi struktury v sovetskom obshchestve* (Sverdlovsk, 1967), pp. 36–43.

[66] *Rabochii klass Sibiri, 1961–1980 g.g.* (Novosibirsk, 1986).

[67] *Rabochii klass SSSR (1951–1965 g.g.)* (Moscow, 1969).

[68] T. H. Rigby, *Communist Party Membership in the USSR, 1917–1967* (Princeton, 1968).

[69] T. H. Rigby, 'Khrushchev and the Rules of the Soviet Political Game', in R. F. Miller and F. Féhér, eds, *Khrushchev and the Communist World* (London, 1984), pp. 39–81.

[70] Leonard Schapiro, *The Communist Party of the Soviet Union* (London, 1971).

[71] R. J. Service, 'The Road to the Twentieth Party Congress: An Analysis

of the Events Surrounding the Central Committee Plenum of July 1953', *Soviet Studies*, vol. xxxiii, no. 2, 1981, pp. 232–45.

[72] Robert Service, 'De-Stalinisation in the USSR Before Khrushchev's Secret Speech', in Francesca Gori, ed., *Il XX Congresso del Pcus* (Milan, 1988), pp. 287–310.

[73] Michael Shafir, 'Eastern Europe', in Martin McCauley, ed., *Khrushchev and Khrushchevism* (London, 1987), pp. 156–79.

[74] Petr Siuda, unpublished interview with David Mandel, 1988.

[75] G. Smirnov, 'Revolyutsionnaya sut' obnovleniya', *Pravda*, 13 March 1987.

[76] G. A. E. Smith, 'Agriculture', in Martin McCauley, ed., *Khrushchev and Khrushchevism* (London, 1987), pp. 95–117.

[77] V. I. Starodub, *Tekhnicheski progress i trud zhenshchin*. Candidate Dissertation, Leningradskii Finansovo-ekonomicheskii Institut im. N. A. Voznesenskogo (Leningrad, 1966).

[78] *Statistika byudzhetov vremeni trudyashchikhsya* (Moscow, 1967).

[79] Tibor Szamuely, 'The Elimination of Opposition Between the Sixteenth and Seventeenth Congresses of the CPSU', *Soviet Studies*, vol. xvii, no. 3, 1966, pp. 318–38.

[80] Michel Tatu, *Power in the Kremlin: From Khrushchev's Decline to Collective Leadership* (London, 1969).

[81] Heinz Timmermann, 'Chruschtschow und das kommunistische Parteiensystem', in Francesca Gori, ed., *Il XX Congresso del Pcus* (Milan, 1988), pp. 269–85.

[82] *Trud v SSSR. Statisticheskii sbornik* (Moscow, 1968).

[83] *Trudovye resursy SSSR (Problemy raspredeleniya i ispol'zovaniya)* (Moscow, 1961).

[84] Stephen White, *Gorbachev and After* (Cambridge, 1992).

Index